Cambridge Elements ≡

Elements in Leadership
edited by
Ronald E. Riggio
Claremont McKenna College
Susan E. Murphy
University of Edinburgh
Founding Editor
Georgia Sorenson
University of Cambridge

ETHICAL LEADERSHIP IN CONFLICT AND CRISIS

Evidence from Leaders on How to Make More Peaceful, Sustainable, and Profitable Communities

Jason Miklian
Centre for Development and the Environment, University of Oslo

John E. Katsos
American University of Sharjah, Queen's University Belfast

CAMBRIDGE
UNIVERSITY PRESS

Shaftesbury Road, Cambridge CB2 8EA, United Kingdom

One Liberty Plaza, 20th Floor, New York, NY 10006, USA

477 Williamstown Road, Port Melbourne, VIC 3207, Australia

314–321, 3rd Floor, Plot 3, Splendor Forum, Jasola District Centre, New Delhi – 110025, India

103 Penang Road, #05–06/07, Visioncrest Commercial, Singapore 238467

Cambridge University Press is part of Cambridge University Press & Assessment, a department of the University of Cambridge.

We share the University's mission to contribute to society through the pursuit of education, learning and research at the highest international levels of excellence.

www.cambridge.org
Information on this title: www.cambridge.org/9781009500715

DOI: 10.1017/9781009446891

First published 2024

A catalogue record for this publication is available from the British Library.

ISBN 978-1-009-50071-5 Hardback
ISBN 978-1-009-44690-7 Paperback
ISSN 2631-7796 (online)
ISSN 2631-7788 (print)

Ethical Leadership in Conflict and Crisis

Evidence from Leaders on How to Make More Peaceful, Sustainable, and Profitable Communities

Elements in Leadership

DOI: 10.1017/9781009446891
First published online: May 2024

Jason Miklian
Centre for Development and the Environment, University of Oslo

John E. Katsos
American University of Sharjah, Queen's University Belfast

Author for correspondence: Jason Miklian, Jason.miklian@sum.uio.no

Abstract: How can business leaders navigate through a world of polycrisis? This work blends historical lessons, firsthand accounts, and ethical perspectives on crisis to fill a key gap in our understanding of effective, ethical leadership through settings of crisis, conflict and/or fragility. Pulling from historical events and contemporary research, this Element looks past individual crises and explores a world of overlapping, permanent crises, or "polycrisis." It contrasts traditional leadership responses with values of community and authenticity, emphasizing the necessity of ethical and servant leadership when conventional business strategies fail. This work offers insights for anyone interested in understanding and navigating the complex landscape of crisis and strategizes enduring leadership for constant crises. This title is also available as Open Access on Cambridge Core.

Keywords: ethical leadership, business ethics, polycrisis, peace and conflict, narrative research

ISBNs: 9781009500715 (HB), 9781009446907 (PB), 9781009446891 (OC)
ISSNs: 2631-7796 (online), 2631-7788 (print)

Contents

Preface

We see a growing divide in business and management research today. It's a gap between studies rooted in empirical findings and books that focus on narrative storytelling. The former are typically academic articles that rarely get read by leaders and can be almost impenetrable to non-specialists. The latter are often pigeonholed as business self-help books, what many of us (rather derisively) refer to as "airport books." They tend to employ a few great anecdotes as proof of a new vision that can solve any leadership challenge, as if it were that easy.

Why is this a problem? Because it encourages the perception that leadership literature is either too dense to be engaging or too superficial to be useful. Therefore, this work aims to reduce this gap in business and management research, especially for younger leaders and students just beginning to navigate this vast literature. We feel that the Cambridge Elements Series on Leadership is the right place for this kind of experimentation.

We aim to show how leaders navigated their way through conflicts and crises to make better companies and better communities. Sometimes they succeeded. Sometimes they failed. But together, their experiences teach us practical lessons and how to apply cutting-edge research to the real world. Our goal is not merely to inform, but to extend the boundary of what a business study can do. It doesn't confine itself to the structural rigidity of an academic journal article or trade book but attempts to hold the interest – and spur the curiosity – of the corporate titan, the academic researcher, and the inquisitive student of any age.

The unique character of this Element is its storytelling as encapsulated in case vignettes, many of which are the product of extensive qualitative research. We present the essentials of these cases to maintain a narrative flow while connecting them to empirical findings. This means we often write from the narrative perspective of the leaders we describe, inferring what they were thinking based on available evidence.

As you follow us through the critical decisions of leaders in their journeys, we hope that it shows how academic research on polycrisis can deliver meaningful learning. For academic researchers, we hope to expand the possibilities of how we engage the broader public in the critical lessons of scholarship through narrative storytelling. For leaders of organizations, we hope to show that the lessons of empirically strong scholarship can be understood without losing their nuance. After all, the best stories are rooted in the reality of everyday life, with all its mistakes, hopefulness, and varying shades of gray.

1 Welcome to a World of Polycrisis

The King of Crisis[1]

The brash genius waved away his useless subordinate, standing across his thick mahogany desk. Another mid-level manager harping on about precarious finances was the last thing he needed on this crisp autumn morning. Five more managers lined up along the wall for their own telling-off. His desk overflowed with the finest gold baubles and the newest dazzling communication inventions. It was the fuck-off desk of a corporate titan.

The genius could never convince his anxious accountants that in the startup world, massive risks made the company – and the man (always, in his view, a man). He'd built his business from nothing more than a brain full of ideas into a household name in seven years. He drove the newest global technologies – on his terms. Everyone knew that most of the change-the-world startups in this field would go bust in a year or two, but the winners would control the market for America's infrastructure for decades.

But the macroeconomic scene had turned hazy over the last eighteen months: Competitors piled up huge losses from dealing with epic fires and other once-a-century disasters that seemed to come from every direction and out of nowhere. The genius whet his lips in anticipation – someone else's misfortune was always a good chance to grow market share.

It was time for another gamble.

His tendency to make big bets that paid off tenfold entranced the nation and made him one of America's richest men. Outsiders saw a man "reclusive, peculiar in dress, authoritarian ... and [having] a towering ego." He preferred to call himself a visionary. Punters dropped their life savings into the company of the man with the Midas touch. The economics of his newest investments didn't really add up, but who cared? He was building an empire.

The genius convinced himself and many others that his companies would sail unscathed through the multiple, simultaneous crises that affected the market. He advised the President, who assured the genius that he was too big to fail. He even gave the President a secret personal loan. He buttered up politicians over dinners at his 53-room mansion to maintain his company's favorable status. He got the government to limit and punish his competitors.

---

[1] Sources used in this section include: Cooke, Jay, 1905. *The Journal of Jay Cooke, or the Gibraltar Records*, Ohio State University Press (1935 ed); Oberholtzer, EP, 1968. *Jay Cooke, Financier of the Civil War (2 Vol.)*, New York: August M. Kelly; Lubetkin, MJ, 2014. *Jay Cooke's Gamble: The Northern Pacific, the Sioux, and the Great Panic of 1873*. Norman: University of Oklahoma Press; New York Times, 1907. "Jay Cooke's Life." November 9. John Adams Institute, 2023. "The Rise of Jay Cooke." www.john-adams.nl/the-rise-of-jay-cooke/, accessed November 6, 2023.

Then came an unexpected disaster that no one could escape: a viral epidemic that brought the nation's transport system to a halt. Trying to blunt the damage, politicians played fast and loose with policy, but it just made things worse. Lonely economists yelled into the void that the economy was at risk of a major collapse.

The genius's max-leverage business model, which worked fine in good economic times when credit flowed readily, suddenly hung by a thread. Convinced of his own abilities, he refused to listen to others in the company who worked with local communities, people terrified of what they were being told on the ground. Panicking, they begged the genius to change course. He laughed off their cowardice.

At 11 AM, a courier arrived, dropping off an urgent telegram. Then another. Then another. The genius read the messages and collapsed in his plush chair. Next came the regional managers, department managers, and seemingly everyone who made any decisions in the company. The reports washed over his ears one by one; he only gave a vacant stare in reply. He told his employees to pack up every inch of his office, which they did, waiting for him to pull one last rabbit out of his hat.

Finally, the genius stood up. He walked out of his office, through his halls of expensive paintings and statues, as the white-collar mob chased his tail. When he got to the front doors, he waited for everyone to exit the building. He then pulled a golden key out of his pocket and locked the doors forever.

Within a week, the company went from the top of the world to the dustbin of history, triggering a domino effect in the banking and technology industries that had relied on him staying afloat. The punters lost everything.

Within a month, three million people were out of a job.

Within a year, a global depression – triggered by the erstwhile genius' hubris – slammed every advanced economy in the world.

A familiar story perhaps. Ken Lay of Enron in 1999? Richard Fuld of Lehman Brothers in 2008? Fanfiction about Elon Musk's Tesla in 2025? No.

This is the story of Jay Cooke and the Northern Pacific Railway – in 1873.

Cooke got mega-rich betting on the new technology of railroads, using the latest inventions at his disposal like the private telegraph to tap into markets faster than anyone else. Cooke, like so many leaders before and since, thought his success could insulate him from crisis. He thought wrong. First, the Great Chicago Fire of 1871 wiped out large chunks of the most important rail transit hub in the US, and then the equine flu of 1872 ground all horse transportation to a halt from government-mandated stops on all transport in and out of New York.

Had Cooke simply listened to employees telling him that rail traffic was dropping precipitously, he could have pivoted to a more solvent financial model. He never did, assuming that, because he'd made it through one crisis unscathed, he had the magic formula to succeed through any challenge. What took Cooke down was his assumption that each crisis was singular. He failed to understand that polycrisis – the convergence of multiple crises simultaneously – requires a different preparation and response. Every crisis not only creates new opportunities but also holds new risks.

Incidentally, Cooke's collapse was just the break an up-and-coming thirty-six-year-old financier needed to take his place, a suave and deeply prepared analyst with a deft ear for community knowledge. His name? John Pierpont ("J.P.") Morgan. While Cooke tripled down on the railroads, Morgan saw the bubble and built international ties to withstand any downturn. Next, he bought Thomas Edison's new electric company. After Cooke went bust, Morgan bought his assets for pennies on the dollar. Once the crisis passed, Morgan used the gains to take Edison's genius nationwide. They called it General Electric, a company we will return to later in this Element.

A World of Polycrisis

Most business and leadership studies assume crises as *events* that leaders must *overcome*. Our research takes a different approach. We explore the spaces where crisis is a *context* that leaders must *navigate*.[2] Polycrisis constitutes "interwoven and overlapping crises" characterized by a "complex intersolidarity of problems, antagonisms, crises, uncontrollable processes, and the general crisis of the planet."[3] While anyone can be lucky enough to steer a firm through a single crisis, succeeding in a world of polycrisis requires leaders to reconceptualize what it means to be a business actor in society.

And make no mistake, we are all living in a polycrisis world. Seismic shifts in the global order are causing unprecedented domino effects. Today we stand at the precipice of three converging and potentially catastrophic trends: climate change, globalization, and growing inequality. On their own, each of these makes the occasional crisis worse. We might see a more destructive hurricane, a more widespread financial meltdown, or more violent civil unrest. But pile these trends on top of another, and together, you end up with a world that is in a longstanding, permanent state of crisis. Today's polycrisis environment carries vast and complex ramifications, with every firm, large and small,

---

[2] See Newstead & Riggio (2023) for a thorough discussion and examples on the evolving definition of "crisis" in business scholarship.

[3] Defined by Morin & Kern (1999).

susceptible to its impacts. Polycrisis is now our reality, an ecosystem that we must survive through and work within.

Looking at our shared experiences with COVID-19 is illuminating. COVID-19 is a coronavirus. So are most strains of the common cold. Because of globalization, this strain spread like lightning across the earth, mutating dozens of times in the process. Because of inequality – of income, of governance, of access to healthcare – the disparities between and within countries were extreme, often ruining the vulnerable while barely bothering the mega-rich, and breeding mass resentment.[4] And because of climate change, more intense natural disasters increased the rate of infection by 180 percent in affected communities.[5]

Pandemics have swept the world before. They're predictable. Indeed, virologists have been warning of a pandemic like COVID-19 for decades. Yet the upheaval of 2020–2021 caught most business leaders completely by surprise. As a result, many leaders flailed in their responses. Many used it as an excuse to fire workers, to close facilities permanently and cancel contracts. Others used it as an excuse to become insular and selfish. Even now, most consider COVID-19 resolved but haven't incorporated its most important lessons into their strategy and planning. When the next crisis hits, we'll hear the same excuses from the unprepared about why they failed, acted unethically, or both. We know what happens to firms that follow that path. Layoffs. Bankruptcy. Implosion.

And there's no relief from crisis just around the corner. The three horsemen of our current age – climate change, globalization, and inequality – are only going to get worse, in part because entrenched interests profit from their perpetuation. But it's also because people have an innate reflex to bury their heads in the sand. Who has time to think of all the one-in-a-thousand crises, let alone spend time to prepare against them all? Collectively, we get shocked when they occur as sociopolitical changes seem to be frozen, and then thaw instantly with a massive, accelerated shock. Think of the collapse of an economy, a coup d'état, or a massive military intervention. The impacts seem rather dramatic to outsiders as they scream from blaring breaking news headlines about the crisis that "no one saw coming."

If one knows where to look, though, one could identify the small changes over time that make a country (and any organization) less resilient, more divided, and more susceptible to chaos. The same is true with companies. In the face of crisis – be it of a political, technological,[6] climatic, economic, or social nature – unprepared firms and their leaders often have few good options.

---

[4] See for example, Murshed (2022).   [5] (de Vries & Rambabu, 2021).

[6] While technology, digital security, and its springboard effects (like the disruptive roles of hacking and artificial intelligence) can have profound creationary impacts upon crisis, we consider a deep discussion as to be beyond the core focus here. That said, we believe that such crises are also applicable to our broader framework and merit additional study. See also discussion in Section 5.

Our current polycrisis environment might be the greatest sociopolitical challenge that companies have ever faced. It impacts companies big and small, local and global. We see it in supply shortages that go from short-term inconveniences to years-long disruptions or power outages that last for weeks or social unrest over injustices. Millions of leaders are desperate to do the right thing, but they struggle to take decisive action because the ways leaders have responded to past crises seem no longer applicable. This is in part because crisis tests the investments that people make in each other: their employees, their customers, and their communities. And only those few that truly know their communities thrive in the end.

Without both strategy *and* community, failure abounds in polycrisis.

Our research over the last fifteen years has uncovered common leadership strategies to not only survive in polycrisis but also to thrive ethically. Transitioning to this new model is hard work for leaders and their organizations. Our evidence shows how it can improve long-term profits *and* bring social benefits. Companies using the lessons we will outline made a host of positive contributions to their local communities. They created value not just for themselves but for all of us. As the world moves deeper into an era of accelerating instability, the best way to understand effective leadership is to learn from those who have succeeded through polycrisis. And history shows us that boldness is a proven strategy for making it through exceptional times only when paired with community engagement.[7]

Succeeding in today's world also requires a shift in our understanding of leadership. Traditional archetypes of robust, seasoned leaders are less compatible in the face of multiplied adversity and instability. Instead, deeply embedded businesses that take principled stands lead organizations through the crisis better. They are the entities operating on the edge of chaos, providing fresh insights and perspectives on leadership during crises. Their stories, struggles, and successes form compelling narratives, and we highlight them in this Element to not only move scholarship forward, but also to inspire and empower leaders to survive and even thrive amidst crises.

This Element showcases what worked for leaders who thrived through polycrisis. Its lessons are rooted in the experiences of the hundreds of leaders that we've interviewed in some of the world's most violent and insecure places, from discussions with leading practitioners and scholars, and researching hundreds of businesses thriving, scraping by, or crumbling as they faced a broad range of violent and nonviolent political and social conflicts. We discovered that successful companies contributed to their local communities more than their

---

[7] Koselleck, 1988; Roitman, 2022.

peers. In some places they helped stop wars. Whether the companies were small entrepreneurial ventures or large multinationals, they engaged with society in a remarkably similar way across countries and organizations.

We made other counter-intuitive discoveries, as well, including that younger leaders navigated perilous waters more successfully than old-timers. Most assume that experienced businesspeople have hard-won insights to lead a firm through crisis. But our research on small businesses during COVID-19 uncovered that owners eighteen to twenty-five years old were the *most* likely to survive through the pandemic, and firms led by owners fifty-five and over were the most likely to close.[8] What does Gen Z know about surviving through a crisis that its Boomer cohorts don't? Even more intriguing, what else are we missing, and who else should we be listening to?

Contained within these pages are answers to these questions. Not just tales of disaster and doom, but also stories of resilience and hope. Crisis implies both danger and opportunity. It is during these periods of profound instability where lessons from those in turbulent circumstances provide value to leaders and leadership researchers. This work also brings their inspiring stories to light to give hard-earned lessons to practitioners and students.

Leadership, Business, and Crisis

Since the establishment of the corporation, social, political, and economic crises have influenced corporate strategy. Corporations and crisis are closely linked, whether we look at Schumpeter's concept of creative destruction, Marx's ideas on overproduction and catastrophe under capitalism, or contemporary work on small company and crisis studies.[9]

One argument is that nimble, decisive action by a courageous leader is key to weathering crisis, carrying echoes of the so-called "Great Man" theory of leadership that dominated scholarship before the mid-twentieth century. Advocates of this approach tend to assume that a crisis is a singular event that happens, requires a response, and is then hopefully followed by a return to business as usual. Some executives believe that when their companies are fighting to survive, ethical leadership is a luxury, while others get mired in questions of which ethics and whose ethics are most

---

[8] Miklian et al., 2021.

[9] See Schumpeter (1942), Clarke (1990), and Herbane (2010). Further, traditional strategy is disrupted by crises (Perrow, 2011), but their onset and scope are unpredictable (Ansell & Boin, 2019; Morgan et al., 2022), generating uncertainties that have fundamental repercussions on key business concepts and can significantly reorganize both company and society (Li & Tallman, 2011). See Miklian & Hoelscher (2022) and Maalouf et al. (2024) for more on the business-crisis relationship.

important to prioritize. Yet another approach is to use avoidance mechanisms, such as promising but never delivering solutions, in hopes that the crisis will simply go away.[10]

Leadership research and managerial ethics under crisis have long studied these relationships. Thus, we define a "manager" in business as any individual with decision-making responsibilities and capabilities in crisis settings, and a "leader" as someone who articulates that responsibility into future-oriented action.[11] This can be decisions for internal relations (like with employees), external relations (such as roles in society), or operational actions (like supply chains or strategy). While we typically think of C-suite executives playing leadership roles, our cases show how country managers, local operational actors, and other employees can also be leaders in polycrisis. In short, all managers can be leaders, and leaders need not be managers. For smaller businesses like family firms and entrepreneurial ventures, a single individual may play all these roles.

Recently, crisis response and adaptation have emerged as key themes in leadership research, especially after COVID-19. Responsible leadership, transformational leadership, and stakeholder theory all offer relevant lenses for studying leadership in crisis and/or conflict contexts.[12] Of particular interest is in the relationship between *leadership ethics* – the "study of the ethical issues related to leadership and the ethics of leadership" – and *ethical leadership* – those actions and relationships that articulate, promote, and operationalize ethical conduct.[13] Under polycrisis, we will show how behavioral consequences focus ethics like a prism. Ethical actions have outsized benefit and visibility, and unethical actions have outsized detrimental consequences. Polycrisis does not change ethical equations; it exacerbates their impact. Thus, we also extract the lessons of stakeholder theory, which emphasizes the critical importance of the

---

[10] See Cawthon (1996), Bauman (2011), and Spector (2016).

[11] See Newstead & Riggio (2023) for an articulation of the implications of "leader" vs. "manager" aggregation / disaggregation under crisis for research.

[12] See Marques et al. (2018) and Newstead & Riggio (2023). Responsible leadership emphasizes the role of business leaders in society in addressing challenges through ethical decision-making, stakeholder engagement, and sustainability (Pless & Maak, 2011). Traits of effective crisis leaders include attending to employee well-being, taking charge, and sustaining morale (Caringal-Go et al., 2021). Research on transformational leadership guiding through crisis is also relevant, characterized by charisma, inspiration, intellectual stimulation, and vision sharing (Rowley et al., 2021). Transformational leaders provide inspiration by communicating their role in a larger mission, creating a supportive social environment (Joniaková et al., 2021).

[13] (Ciulla, 1995) On ethical leadership, see Trevno et al. (2000), Brown et al. (2005), Brown & Treviño (2006), Zhu et al. (2016), and Riggio (ed.) (2019). On leadership ethics see Ciulla (2003, 2004). On distinctions and further leadership research see Seeger & Ulmer (2001), Bauman (2011), Alpaslan & Mitroff (2021), Yeo & Jeon (2021), Wilson & Newstead (2022). Our thanks to anonymous reviewer 1 for the guidance on these points.

interests and needs of internal and external stakeholders to help leaders enhance information visibility, collaboration, and supply chain resilience in a socially responsible way.[14] This work bridges academic literature in transformational leadership and stakeholder theory, unpacking how ethical leadership manifests in polycrisis.

We also aim to help fill a key conceptual gap on a topic that increasingly defines our world: What happens when a company experiences many crises at once? Our world today is one of systemic, overlapping crisis, filled with the sorts of "grand challenges" and "wicked problems" that seemingly used to come only once a in generation. These problems, including climate change, democratic backsliding, and rising inequality, are too big and complex for one business, government, or country to solve alone. In the past, wicked problems tended to come at a more manageable pace. Think of how we came together to reduce our (self-made) ozone hole in Antarctica in the 1980s or the dramatic global reduction in malaria over the past century.

But today, humanity faces multiple grand challenges at once. It doesn't just strain resources and attention spans, but our psychological ability to feel resilient. At a personal level, it can make us feel like these sorts of problems are not solvable. We give up or perhaps try to ignore them altogether. But a business doesn't have the luxury of hiding its head in the sand. It *must* navigate through wicked problems and grand challenges just in order to survive.

Unfortunately, cutting-edge business and management research has been slow in guiding leaders that want to learn how to prepare. These issues should be the cornerstone of research today, but less than 3 percent of top business and management academic articles critically assess grand challenges or wicked problems. Why? In short, because the issues are so big it's hard to deliver findings that are expansive enough to address the problem, yet specific enough to be actionable. The situation is so dire that some have called for a completely new structural and economic paradigm for business schools as the only way that we can re-prioritize education and scholarship on what *really* matters to succeed in these environments.[15]

---

[14] This is a large field that we cannot do justice to in a single paragraph, but note of particular interest (Parmar et al., 2010; Obrenovic et al., 2020; Gigol et al., 2021; Dubey, 2022). To wit, in literatures on leadership (Treviño et al., 2003; Svedin, 2011; Coldwell, 2017) and crisis management (Simola, 2003; Sparrowe, 2005; Yeoh & Jeon, 2022), the relationship between ethical leadership and crisis management is often taken as a presumption. Although some scholars have developed theoretical foundation-building, moving from anecdotal to empirical evidence is the next step (Katsos & Fort, 2016).

[15] For further reading, see Harley, B., & Fleming, P. (2021). Not even trying to change the world: Why do elite management journals ignore the major problems facing humanity? *The Journal of Applied Behavioral Science*, *57*, 133–152; Dorado, S., Antadze, N., Purdy, J., & Branzei, O. (2022). Standing on the shoulders of giants: Leveraging management research on grand challenges. *Business & Society*, *61*, 1242–1281; Daviter, F. (2019). Policy analysis in the face

Top public outlets like *Harvard Business Review* have an even bigger challenge. These publications have ramped up their discussions of grand challenges in response to demands from terrified business strategists. But they have even fewer words to capture big ideas, and specificity is usually the first casualty when cutting for space. Those wishing to learn more about what to *actually* do are left wanting.[16]

So, let's dig into the details, starting with the term "polycrisis" itself, and how it helps us picture what a "grand challenge" or a "wicked problem" can be. Polycrisis has "four core properties: extreme complexity, high nonlinearity, transboundary causality, and deep uncertainty." It conceptualizes crisis not as event but as a condition, and has struck a chord globally, including in the European Union, business press, and consultancy spheres.[17] It's also entered into the mainstream: "At the World Economic Forum, polycrisis became the buzzword for financiers, politicians and policymakers searching for a way to talk about 'business as usual' in a dramatically changing world."[18] The Financial Times called it 2022's word of the year: "Welcome to the world of the polycrisis, (where) today desperate shocks interact so that the whole is worse than the sum of the parts."[19]

Polycrises describe not just the sheer number of crises, but an environment of instability that seems to never end. This can be from multiple overlapping crises that come in waves, as Lebanon has experienced over the past forty years. Or it can mean a number of socioeconomic shocks that all arrive at once, like many fragile countries experienced during the COVID-19 pandemic. Polycrisis literature imagines fragile places where crisis is the rule rather than the exception, much like complexity theory.[20]

As the concept has acquired popularity, it's most frequently employed to further our comprehension of how climate change interacts with other crises as

---

of complexity: What kind of knowledge to tackle wicked problems? *Public Policy and Administration, 34*(1), 62–83; Brammer, S., Branicki, L., Linnenluecke, M., & Smith, T. (2019). Grand challenges in management research: Attributes, achievements, and advancement. *Australian Journal of Management, 44*(4), 517–533; Waddock, S. (2020). Will businesses and business schools meet the grand challenges of the era? *Sustainability.* https://doi .org/10.3390/su12156083.

[16] We very much include ourselves and our own publications for HBR in this cohort of articles that addressed the topic yet couldn't wrangle enough space to be specific. Ultimately, it's the sort of topic that needs more book-length explorations as opposed to 1,500-word summaries.

[17] Junker, 2018; Piereder et al., 2022; Tooze, 2022; PwC, 2023.   [18] Knight et al., 2023.

[19] Financial Times (2022a, 2022b).

[20] Sources for this paragraph includes Bratianu (2020), Joseph et al. (2020), and Katsos & Miklian (2021). Also note that the expansion of spatial frameworks (Martin et al., 2022), chaordic systems analysis (Pappas, 2018), collaborative knowledge exchange (Farley et al., 2023), and cooperative institution building (Mullings & Otuomagie, 2023) constitute emerging strategies to navigate polycrisis.

a threat multiplier and threat accelerator, exacerbating institutional stress in economic and political systems.[21] The Cascade Institute offers an informative (if disheartening) look at one such polycrisis event: Russia's invasion of Ukraine and the climate crisis:

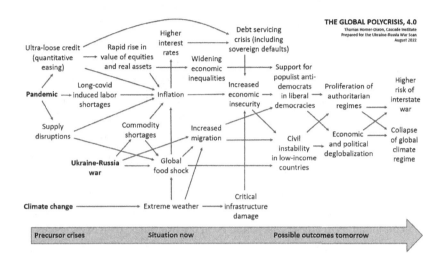

This scenario reflects the need for models that incorporate polycrisis. Crisis management strategies stress preparation for all possible negative impacts. But it would be impossible for even the most resource-rich firm to adequately prepare for all of the above risks and threats, let alone their consequences. To break this seemingly Gordian knot, is there another way to lead that applies across the crisis ecosystem? Because "there must be a point when crisis-as-context ceases to be a crisis at all and instead becomes a fundamental feature of the system."[22] We argue that polycrisis constitutes an opportunity for leaders to consider their business' place within sociopolitical systems as collaborative endeavors.

But how have successful leaders employed common strategies in times of polycrisis? If they have, how did they differ from what crisis "best practice" might have suggested? Perhaps most importantly, can we pinpoint the emergence of new strategies for leadership and crisis in a fundamentally new global environment? This Element aims to answer these questions.

---

[21] (Swilling, 2013, 2019; Hoyer et al., 2023).

[22] The role of crisis in innovation (Eggers, 2020; Nikiforou et al., 2023) and in sociopolitical institutional transformation (Cordero, 2016; compass, 2017) has been well described in management and crisis studies literature. Other sources for this paragraph include Pearson & Mitroff (1993), Mitroff (2007), Knight et al. (2023), Newstead & Riggio (2023).

About This Element

This work is built on three sets of findings. First, we extracted findings from fifteen years of research on business in crisis zones and conflict settings. We employed a variety of methods in our research, prioritizing deep qualitative fieldwork. We have conducted interviews in-person with over 350 business owners in conflict-affected regions since 2009, including in the Democratic Republic of Congo, Syria, Ukraine, Cyprus, Yemen, Venezuela, Liberia, Myanmar, Iraq, Colombia, Sri Lanka, and Lebanon, and online interviews with managers in Ukraine, Zimbabwe, Sri Lanka, and the Palestinian Territories. We conducted studies of CEOs, managers, and smaller businesses and entrepreneurs in Libya, Syria, Palestine, Iraq, Colombia, and Indonesia as well as quantitative country/region case studies and grassroots stakeholder systems analyses, publishing dozens of academic articles on these topics. Scholars and curious readers can see Appendix A for our methodology and limitations.

We also interviewed nearly one thousand citizens living in conflict and crisis zones, having the privilege to hear their experiences of business engagement with communities in crisis. This cohort is on the frontlines, with experiences of loss and triumph that we aim to honor. This Element brings these lessons to one place for the first time.

Our first set of findings is in Section 2. Here, we show how conceptions of ethical, moral, and lawful leadership of a firm come under strain during polycrisis, pulling leaders in varied directions from best practices that become incompatible with ethical behavior. We show how guidance was developed for a world with singular (or no) crises, and how this guidance becomes less useful in a polycrisis environment. We also show that, while firms aim to nurture trust with employees, consumers, and the public in crisis situations, this trust cannot be bought or certified, it must be earned through the time-consuming work of building responsible sociopolitical relationships. Here we answer questions like why do the responses to uncertainty that we're told will make everything better fail us when we need them most?

Our second set of findings are presented in Section 3. Here, we show that leaders who understand their sociopolitical context are more likely to succeed. Our research shows how companies that had little or only cursory engagement with local communities, viewing them merely as sources of consumers or raw materials, were unlikely to outrun upheaval. Shutting out the local community during crisis multiplied the risk that the project at hand, or even the company itself, would fail. And the most surprisingly effective partnerships of all? Teaming up with competitors. Here we address questions like: Why is growing uncertainty and crisis the key problem in business operations and strategic planning? How will it get worse, and why are we so sure?

Our third set of findings is presented in Section 4. Companies must not be afraid to take principled stands, even political ones. They must also work not just with, but beyond governments or elected officials when public institutions are inadequate or thwart progress. Our research shows that firms thrived when they made consistent choices and communicated them clearly, even if parts of the population disagreed. We address questions like: Why must leadership and company culture incorporate the reality of constant crisis to succeed? What do truly ethical companies look like, and why are they more profitable? How can a crisis-proof culture be built in the US or European Union by learning from war-zone success stories?

Our final Section 5 provides a discussion of our empirical work, connecting it back to cutting-edge theory on ethical leadership. We offer a roadmap for the multiples of business action in polycrisis, highlighting how success isn't a matter of luck, but requires a broader understanding of the role of business in, of, and for society.

2 Why "Best Practice" Fails During Crisis

99% Sustainable[23]

Nestled next to an ancient lake on the island of Sumatra, Indonesia lies a bespoke plantation. The volcanic soil is so rich around Lake Toba that coffee bushes here grow the world's most prized and delicious beans. Buyers for Starbucks discovered this gem over a decade ago, scooping it up to package a limited-edition line for $75 a pound. Every batch sold out like lightning. Starbucks shared the profits with growers, enriching the local population beyond their wildest imaginations in a part of the world where other farmers earned just $3 a day.

But when Starbucks entered Lake Toba, they excluded a powerful community actor. The region that they hoped to transform with coffee was linked to an extensive network of criminals with a lot to lose: the rubber mafia. It wasn't that Starbucks didn't know of their existence; they'd been buying elsewhere in Sumatra for over a decade. But in Lake Toba, rubber and coffee farmhands ran in the same circles, with all aware that rubber – not coffee – ruled the region. The mafia had an iron grip over local politics, built over a generation alongside rubber barons. Anyone who threatened this model, be it a local politician, farmer, or foreign multinational company with a green mermaid logo, would be a target.

When Starbucks came in with their new sustainable development model, they upended an uneasy truce between farmers and the rubber mafia: the farmers would stay out of politics, and the mafia would leave them alone. "Best practice" policy for Starbucks and other large firms means to exclude, sometimes for legal reasons in the home market and sometimes for perceived ethical reasons, any partners who are deemed at high risk for corruption or who are "politically exposed." Since farmers would earn much more from growing coffee, Starbucks assumed that rational self-interest would prevail, enriching an impoverished community, while also starving the rubber mafia of capital. Employing global best practice CSR models, they then paid a premium for workers to switch from rubber to coffee. This was all part of Starbucks' new model to make every bean they sourced sustainable to C.A.F.E. standards. Lake Toba became their landmark case.

Yet, because Starbucks never engaged with the most powerful local actors – the rubber mafia – it became impossible to ensure that Starbucks' largess durably improved the farmers' lives. Understandably, as the farmers became more wealthy many sought to become more active in local politics. The mafia lashed out at the new threat, destroying farms and threatening assassinations to anyone who dared challenge their control. Some farmers went back to working

---

[23] This case is adapted from Miklian & Katsos (2021c).

the rubber plantations; others gave up farming entirely. When Starbucks returned the next season and discovered that there was nothing to buy, farmers told us that Starbucks had written off the valley as a perplexing loss, never to return.

Today, the Sumatra plantations lie in shambles. Our talks with farmers shared a tragic backdrop: unkempt and barren coffee bushes as far as the eye could see, with scores of abandoned houses littering the otherwise pristine valley. The farmers told us that they hid during the days, fearing execution. With nothing to buy, Starbucks has closed shop and moved on to other valleys in search of next season's bespoke bean.

What Went Wrong?

In our research, we found that companies like Starbucks generally want to do the right thing wherever they operate. But many leaders get it wrong under crisis by following what they are told are "best practices" from experts who take their evidence from non-crisis settings. In polycrisis environments, importing best practices from elsewhere can be disastrous. To understand why Starbucks failed despite following best practice principles, and how a different approach could have generated a more sustainable, profitable, and positive approach, we unpack the additive intersections of ethics, law, and best practice. In this Section, we present four findings: *Why "Best Practice" Breaks Under Polycrisis*; *Whose "Best Practice"?*; *"Legal" Doesn't Mean "Moral" in Polycrisis*; and, *"Legal" Doesn't Mean "Profitable" in Polycrisis*.

To do this, we studied over 16,000 business owners in a half-dozen countries experiencing polycrisis, where community engagement and acting beyond government guidance were essential. Next, we examine the origins of corporate ethical leadership to see how early efforts to make a positive impact on society led some companies to prioritize legal over moral considerations. Then, we'll see how international organizations and business consortia often rely on past experiences that are less applicable to current polycrisis situations. Finally, we'll look at how companies conflate profits with purpose without considering the agendas of lawmakers.

Why "Best Practice" Breaks Under Polycrisis

Broadly understood, "best practice" means following guidelines, standards, or other distilled previous experiences known to deliver positive business outcomes. It incorporates empirically sound principles but is also a guidepost during times of challenge to show employees and consumers that management is doing the best possible job of navigating through difficult times. But what happens when we apply best practice from the typical singular crisis models of scholarship onto a polycrisis environment?[24]

To test these dynamics, we surveyed 16,500 small and medium enterprise (SME) owners and managers in seven dynamic, global cities. We wanted to see how they adjusted to the addition of yet another crisis, COVID-19. In Bogotá (Colombia), Medellín (Colombia), Beirut (Lebanon), Cape Town (South Africa), Caracas (Venezuela), San Pedro Sula (Honduras), and San Salvador (El Salvador)[25] we gleaned insights from both business leaders and citizens about the broad challenges they faced. We asked them questions about their strategy and their engagement with communities and governments. We asked them how COVID-19 affected their businesses, their social actions, and their profitability. What they told us was illuminating.

We found striking commonalities across these very different cities and companies, especially when comparing these results with what "best practice" would have told them to do to survive.

Companies that expanded their community engagement during COVID (e.g., hiring disadvantaged workers, undertaking charity work, assisting the unemployed, helping to reduce local violence) were three times more likely to be profitable than their peers, and *nine* times more likely to survive. Where firms gave more community help, customers were eight times more likely to see them as actors who helped society.

We know from previous research that SMEs are particularly vulnerable to crisis effects.[26] When crises hit, prevailing business models can become ineffective, which is particularly challenging for small firms. But smaller is not

---

[24] Crisis tends to amplify latent fissures, as when the 2008 financial crisis led to a deep crisis of trust in business ethics (Faugère & Gergaud, 2017), leading to a proliferation of regulation in response to corporate governance failures (Price & van der Walt, 2013). While ethical companies can outperform the market both in times of growth and during market decline, firms that implement ethical policies often do so because it is an integral part of their business, rather than as a response to external pressures (Magrizos et al., 2021). For example, COVID-19 pandemic was firms engage in a wide range of ethical expansion, motivated by both utilitarianism and deontological factors (Manuel & Herron, 2020), adapting codes of ethics and prescribed forms of ethical behavior (Eweje & Brunton, 2010). Crises can test ethical frameworks and the extent to which they guide decision-making and behavior, especially when crisis-driven actions differ from pre- or postcrisis priorities (Manuel & Herron, 2020).

[25] Elements of this section adapted from Bull et al. (2021).

[26] For example, larger firms weather crises better than smaller firms (Kitching et al., 2009), with SMEs more negatively impacted (Doern, 2014). SMEs are less able to influence their external environment (Lai et al., 2016), making them more vulnerable to crisis than large firms (Marshall et al., 2015); have a harder time recovering (Chang, 2010); and are more likely to shutter (Sydnor et al., 2017). SMEs face tighter access to capital, lack sufficient managerial capacities, are more dependent on a narrower customer base, and less prepared to navigate disruption than large firms (William & Schaefer, 2013; Piete & Zachary, 2015; Bartik et al., 2020). Other sources for this section include Davidsson (2015), Shepherd & Williams (2019), Bene (2020), and Morgan (2020).

Communities View Businesses
Through the Lens of a Crisis

Where things get better, citizens see businesses as
part of the solution. Where environments deteriorate,
citizens see businesses as harmful actors.

CITIES: BOGOTÁ & MEDELLÍN · BEIRUT · CAPE TOWN · CARACAS · SAN PEDRO SULA · SAN SALVADOR

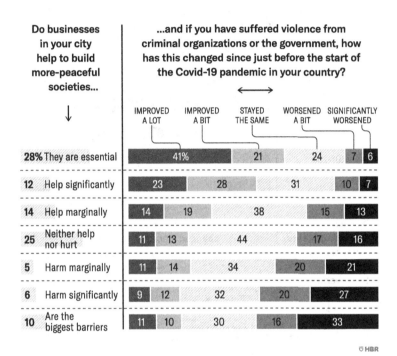

Do businesses in your city help to build more-peaceful societies... ↓	...and if you have suffered violence from criminal organizations or the government, how has this changed since just before the start of the Covid-19 pandemic in your country? ⟵⟶				
	IMPROVED A LOT	IMPROVED A BIT	STAYED THE SAME	WORSENED A BIT	SIGNIFICANTLY WORSENED
28% They are essential	41%	21	24	7	6
12 Help significantly	23	28	31	10	7
14 Help marginally	14	19	38	15	13
25 Neither help nor hurt	11	13	44	17	16
5 Harm marginally	11	14	34	20	21
6 Harm significantly	9	12	32	20	27
10 Are the biggest barriers	11	10	30	16	33

⟲HBR

Figure 1

always weaker. Small and medium enterprises more often exploit new opportunities during crises. However, global crises like COVID-19 may temper such benefits due to societal vulnerability, leading us to consider what unique characteristics may come into play when multiple crises strike.

Government support is often seen as a key survival metric, but our results exposed some interesting contradictions. Only 9 percent of firms received significant COVID-19 aid, while 75 percent received none. Yet, firms that went to informal actors like mafias or armed groups instead were even *more* likely to survive than those that got government aid.

Furthermore, 55 percent of respondents said their firms had recently been threatened with violence or extortion, a finding that held across firm sizes, sectors, and locations. While the initial COVID-19 wave in 2020 led to a reduction in crime in Latin America as communities entered lockdowns, the

Smaller Companies Got the Least Government Assistance During Covid-19

And their businesses suffered because of it.

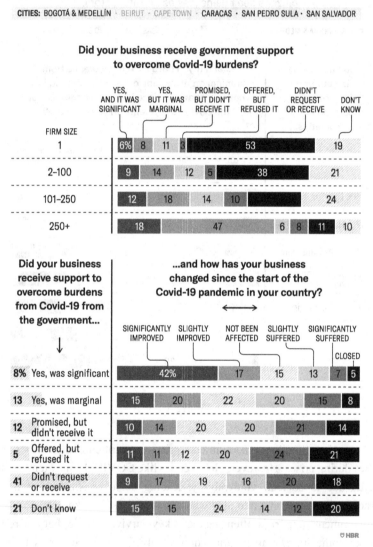

Figure 2

longevity and depth of the crisis triggered a whiplash effect. Extortion figures in some cities went to all-time highs, with a rapid growth in groups exploiting the pandemic to grow their extortion capabilities into the digital sphere.

Our findings show that polycrisis environments are significantly harder for businesses to survive in (an expected result), but also show how understanding

In Cape Town, Younger Generations Are More Likely to See Violence as Justified

A majority of young adults said violence was justified
to protect community interests and keep people safe.

CITIES: BOGOTÁ & MEDELLÍN · BEIRUT · **CAPE TOWN** · CARACAS · SAN PEDRO SULA · SAN SALVADOR

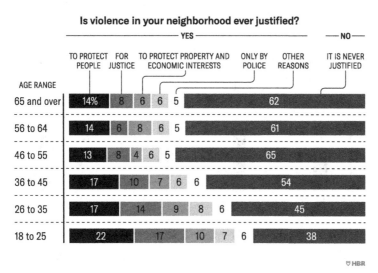

Is violence in your neighborhood ever justified?

AGE RANGE	TO PROTECT PEOPLE	FOR JUSTICE	TO PROTECT PROPERTY AND ECONOMIC INTERESTS		ONLY BY POLICE	OTHER REASONS	IT IS NEVER JUSTIFIED
65 and over	14%	8	6	6	5		62
56 to 64	14	6	8	6	5		61
46 to 55	13	8	4	6	5		65
36 to 45	17	10	7	6	6		54
26 to 35	17	14	9	8	6		45
18 to 25	22	17	10	7	6		38

⊽ HBR

Figure 3

the sociopolitical nature of crisis created more effective response strategies. When companies see their surroundings as the product of outside forces *and* company decision-making that impacts society, they formulate better strategies for polycrisis survival. This contrasts with the more "textbook" best practice model that suggests mimicking a large firm's "ride it out" approach until the crisis passes, which in our findings was a less effective approach.

These findings help to explain *what* firms can do to survive polycrisis. Just as important is *how* they can survive and eventually succeed. We start with the recognition that no two social problems are alike. This is in line with research and practice in peacebuilding and development studies. Incorporating the local context about what is most needed is essential to incorporate successful sociopolitical strategies. For leaders, this means that approaches to crisis management based on instinct alone, which primarily rely on what was experienced before, often fail to provide the most valuable guidance in polycrisis.[27]

---

[27] Ganson et al. (2019) and Kottika et al. (2020).

How Firms Experience Extortion and Violence

Over half of all firms have recently experienced extortion and violence — and smaller firms are the most susceptible.

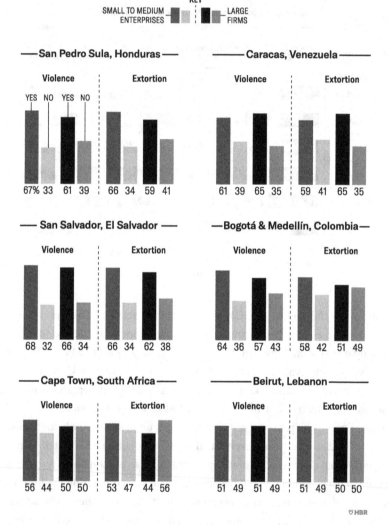

Since the outbreak of Covid-19 in your community, has your business experienced violence or extortion?

Figure 4

Our research of SMEs in fragile cities showed that those who did this were more successful both during and after crisis, and the findings were strongest in those places where polycrisis was most severe. Taken together, the cases show how

In Beirut, Small Businesses Are Perceived to Do More for Their Communities

This may better position them to survive a crisis.

CITIES: BOGOTÁ & MEDELLÍN · **BEIRUT** · CAPE TOWN · CARACAS · SAN PEDRO SULA · SAN SALVADOR

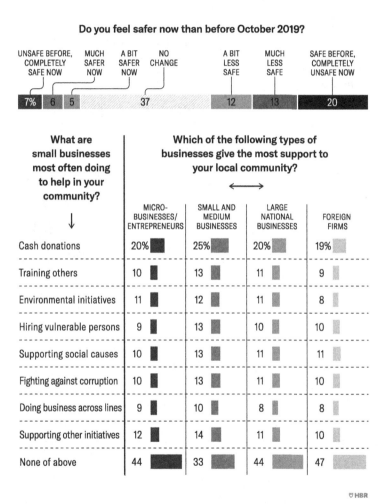

Do you feel safer now than before October 2019?

UNSAFE BEFORE, COMPLETELY SAFE NOW	MUCH SAFER NOW	A BIT SAFER NOW	NO CHANGE	A BIT LESS SAFE	MUCH LESS SAFE	SAFE BEFORE, COMPLETELY UNSAFE NOW
7%	6	5	37	12	13	20

What are small businesses most often doing to help in your community? ↓

Which of the following types of businesses give the most support to your local community? ←→

	MICRO-BUSINESSES/ ENTREPRENEURS	SMALL AND MEDIUM BUSINESSES	LARGE NATIONAL BUSINESSES	FOREIGN FIRMS
Cash donations	20%	25%	20%	19%
Training others	10	13	11	9
Environmental initiatives	11	12	11	8
Hiring vulnerable persons	9	13	10	10
Supporting social causes	10	13	11	11
Fighting against corruption	10	13	11	10
Doing business across lines	9	10	8	8
Supporting other initiatives	12	14	11	10
None of above	44	33	44	47

♡HBR

Figure 5

SMEs and MNCs operate in "the same but different worlds" (and MSMEs in another world still) under polycrisis, thus highlighting the importance of contextual approach to crisis leadership. In short, there's no one "right response" to COVID or a financial crisis for all firms, but a "right method" for firms of all types may exist to help navigate through polycrisis, which we return to in the final Section.

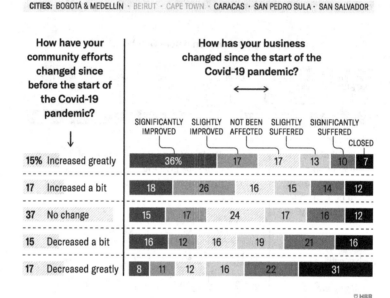

Community Engagement Helps Businesses Through Crisis

Companies that engaged more with their communities during the pandemic were less impacted by the downturn.

CITIES: BOGOTÁ & MEDELLÍN · BEIRUT · CAPE TOWN · CARACAS · SAN PEDRO SULA · SAN SALVADOR

How have your community efforts changed since before the start of the Covid-19 pandemic? ↓

How has your business changed since the start of the Covid-19 pandemic? ←→

	SIGNIFICANTLY IMPROVED	SLIGHTLY IMPROVED	NOT BEEN AFFECTED	SLIGHTLY SUFFERED	SIGNIFICANTLY SUFFERED	CLOSED
15% Increased greatly	36%	17	17	13	10	7
17 Increased a bit	18	26	16	15	14	12
37 No change	15	17	24	17	16	12
15 Decreased a bit	16	12	16	19	21	16
17 Decreased greatly	8	11	12	16	22	31

○ HBR

Figure 6

Whose "Best Practice"?

In crises, many managers are tempted to seek shortcuts to solve complex issues. When the shortcuts are offered by some of the world's most respected organizations, the allure is almost impossible to resist. These organizations often refer to their solutions as "best practice." These often come with the implicit prestige and respect of working with international organizations or global nongovernmental organizations, including certification schemes and corporate responsibility awards that amplify echo chambers.

These initiatives are popular. Dozens of principles claim to help businesses be positive corporate stewards in crisis and conflict, including the United Nations Guiding Principles, corporate governance frameworks, and business and human rights guidelines. Most offer low benchmarks for social responsibility: don't make your employees slaves; don't hire ten-year-olds; and don't dump toxic sludge into villages.

"Best practices" developed through these initiatives end up like that album by the former superstar who's been surrounded by "yes men" for a decade: An

In Cape Town, Community Support Comes from Business

Survey respondents said businesses support the
community more than municipal authorities.

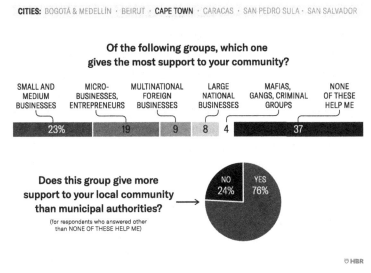

CITIES: BOGOTÁ & MEDELLÍN · BEIRUT · **CAPE TOWN** · CARACAS · SAN PEDRO SULA · SAN SALVADOR

**Of the following groups, which one
gives the most support to your community?**

SMALL AND MEDIUM BUSINESSES	MICRO- BUSINESSES, ENTREPRENEURS	MULTINATIONAL FOREIGN BUSINESSES	LARGE NATIONAL BUSINESSES	MAFIAS, GANGS, CRIMINAL GROUPS	NONE OF THESE HELP ME
23%	19	9	8	4	37

**Does this group give more
support to your local community
than municipal authorities?** →

(for respondents who answered other
than NONE OF THESE HELP ME)

NO 24%   YES 76%

ⓗHBR

Figure 7

unlistenable debacle that leaves the public even less assured of their ability than before. Companies typically pick whichever one best fits their business model and initiate the annual rite of box-ticking their actions. Corporate Social Responsibility (CSR) departments then use the reports to generate impact metrics, making them look on par with accounting and financial numbers to show improvement year over year *ad nauseam*.

They are indeed like accounting figures ... but in the worst ways. Just like how corporate cheats cook the books through shell corporations, dummy transfers, tax havens, and plain old fraud, so too can social responsibility reporters fudge human numbers to make it look like a company is making a positive contribution when the opposite is true. It can make producers of standards look like propagandists, when there's a standard for every business to pluck off the shelf with minimal effort to suit, no matter the sector or location.

As professors who teach a new batch of idealistic business and development students every semester, we often assign one task that never fails to crush their dreams: a review of Values Statements on corporate websites. These statements are so vague as to be useless or outright evil in their duplicity. For example, global tobacco giant Altria (formerly Philip Morris) lists such aspirations as, "We do what's right," "We care for each other," and "We deliver for our consumers and our customers."[28] Quizzical ways indeed to reframe giving people lung cancer and addicting people to deadly products.

As upheavals become more common and complex, firms find themselves embroiled in sociopolitical concerns to an unprecedented degree. Many realize that "best practices" don't help in polycrisis because things will not simply go back to "normal" after the latest pandemics, wildfires, or protests. Business leaders are adept at recognizing sociopolitical change as it happens. But in our interviews, owners and managers from firms large and small, in war zones and the US, repeatedly told us they regretted failing to take the changes seriously to implement a more adaptive business model.

Why did we keep hearing the same laments? One reason is that business strategy prioritizes and rewards reacting to changes, not taking decisive action to prepare. Even a field acutely aware of future threats – information security teams trying to ward off hackers and malicious actors – still faces challenges in balancing these demands.[29] Managers are realizing that political, social, and environmental shifts must get the same attention as operational or competitive threats, as articulated by materiality debates in Environmental, Social and Governance (ESG) discussions. Yet, most managers aren't trained to implement a decision-making model that incorporates exogenous, sociopolitical issues. This is especially true when firms watch countries with similar geographic or socioeconomic settings topple and think of that their "home" systems are somehow inherently better and thus impervious to crisis.

It's tempting to think of this as a signal vs. noise problem: People receive so much information that it's impossible for them to pick the right crisis needle out of a massive info dump haystack. But preparing for crisis is like holding up a giant magnet to the haystack, revealing the needles and extracting them before they can do hidden damage. Once companies realize which social and political problems can impact their operating environments, they can prepare for the most likely ones.

So why do companies continue to pursue these sorts of ceremonial activities that are clearly no more than window dressing? One reason is that to investors and casual observers, they *do* work. Most principles set low targets that are easily achievable or constitute activities the company already does, even if they're just precision-machined marketing. But the real work of preparing for crisis lies in obtaining a social license and social insurance to operate, and those can only be obtained by direct action. Relying on outside standards that mean

---

[28] Altria, 2019 (https://web.archive.org/web/20150914225753mp_/http://www.altria.com/About-Altria/Our-Mission-and-Values/Pages/default.aspx).

[29] Baskerville et al. (2014).

little for local communities doesn't get companies much more than a platform to talk about these issues.

"Best practices" in CSR or business ethics often don't consider local power dynamics on the ground in crisis – a problem that has been evident for at least thirty years.[30] Leaders' insistence on following these guidelines is critical because of findings on ethical leadership that indicate the role that leaders play in organizations and the ethics of their employees. If leaders show their employees that ethics are just window dressing, employees pick up the message quickly with increases in misconduct. It seems unlikely that this response would get better in crisis; in our research with leaders in crisis and conflict zones, these responses usually get more pronounced.

"Legal" Doesn't Mean "Moral" in Polycrisis

Despite the rise of business ethics as a field over the past fifty years, and its application through CSR, Creating Shared Value, ESG frameworks and similar, what we often think of as "new" ideas on business and society have bounced around for hundreds of years in different names and guises. However, one stubborn constant is that leaders often feel under-equipped in their efforts to know what specifically to do to be more ethical, and if what they're doing makes societies better.

One thing that most leaders *do* understand however, is that doing it the wrong way can lead to ruin. Ethical action is often tested to its limit during times of crisis – and firms willing to innovate in such periods are typically more successful and resilient. Adaptive actions to social shifts are a foundational feature of successful firms and are even more essential today with the seemingly universal securitization and polarization of everything in business and society, even while we feel less secure and resilient to crisis than we've ever been.

Much ethical leadership under crisis literature emphasizes the personal moral compasses of the C-suite, and crisis management performance strategies.[31] These sorts of ethical strategies tend to carry a "ride out the storm"-type mentality. But in sociopolitical crisis, taking a long-term perspective and considering the broader consequences of decisions can contribute to more sustainable and responsible business practices. This is because cultural factors like the impact of power dynamics, collectivism, and uncertainty avoidance on

---

[30] (Donaldson & Dunfee, 1994, 2017; Brown et al., 2006; Mayer et al., 2010).

[31] For example, leadership styles and competencies (Bhaduri, 2019a); developing diverse teams with clear, shared goals (Standiford et al., 2021); building employees' resolution efficacy (Babalola et al., 2018); inclusive leaders who invite employee contributions to a caring ethical climate (Qi & Liu, 2017); and reducing ethical ambiguity in decision-making (Cakir et al., 2022).

ethical attitudes can positively influence managers' actions for more respon-sible business ethics.[32]

The focus on legal compliance by companies as a stand-in for moral obliga-tions reflects a growing gap between legal requirements and ethical responsibil-ities during crises, whereby firms that focus on the former as the end goal rather than simply one means to achieve the end (operating profitably and ethically) under-perform.[33] Crises can also bring about increasing regulation because of their own misdeeds, such as when Upton Sinclar's *The Jungle* exposed meat-packing firms and triggered waves of corporate regulations, and the rise of the paternalistic corporation and company towns. Or it can be exogenous, as when Kimberley-Clark switched its factories from making Kleenex to machine guns during World War II.

But in a crisis-rich world, how should leaders act when legal guidance and ethical guidance clash? The empirical gap between legal and ethical best practices can be generations in the making.

For example, in 1926 the American company Firestone obtained a unique concession: A ninety-nine-year lease for land in Liberia that would become the world's largest contiguous rubber plantation. Everything was going swimmingly for Firestone until Liberia's rulers were overthrown in a violent coup in 1980. Over the next twenty-five years, Firestone conducted a master class in neutrality. It ignored human rights violations, including the execution of presidents and cabinet members without trial on national television.

Most infamously, Firestone paid money masquerading as taxes to one of the twentieth century's worst warlords, Charles "Blood Diamond" Taylor. Taylor used Firestone's plantation payments as a cash machine and launching pad for military operations, paying child soldiers, and funding ethnic cleansing and genocide of rival tribes. Taylor was finally removed from Liberia in 2003 and convicted of crimes against humanity at The Hague.

Throughout, Firestone made decisions via company headquarters in Ohio, not in Liberia. They aimed to stay out of politics under all circumstances to keep the rubber flowing. That drive led to lawsuits, work stoppages, and excessive "tax payments," counter-productively generating the very shortages, supply chain disruptions, and violence toward their local employees that they had been trying to avoid. They also became entangled with war criminals and genocide. All along, they followed local law, the best practices of their time,

---

[32] (Okpara, 2014; de Andrade Melim-McLeod, 2018; Choflet et al., 2021).

[33] See Thoms (2008) on codes of ethics, Coldwell (2017) on the value of a moral compass during crises, Carroll (2021) on resetting CSR thinking, and the growing gap between legal require-ments/compliance and ethical responsibilities during crises (Pérez & Bosque, 2014; Baden, 2016; Corral de Zubielqui & Harris, 2023).

and the advice of top business experts. Doing so led to their complicity in a wide range of human rights abuses.

None of this was Firestone's intent; it was just the natural extension of a failed mindset that the lessons of "normal" times apply equally in situations of governance breakdowns and uncertainty. In short, the best practice advice failed for Firestone in polycrisis. And it failed in spite of the best intentions to "get it right" and "do the right thing."

In each of the situations mentioned earlier, companies just trying to follow the law (or some restated version of it) ended up in trouble. The law is a moral minimum, not an ambitious ethical target. The latter is what leaders will need to set for their organizations to lead through polycrisis.

"Legal" Doesn't Mean "Profitable" in Polycrisis

The rich farmlands of eastern Odisha, India, held a similar cautionary lesson for POSCO, one of the world's largest steel companies headquartered in South Korea.[34] Just as with Starbucks and Firestone, POSCO tried to be a force for good. Under the guidance of India head Yong-Won Yoon, POSCO launched a $12 billion steel project in Odisha in 2005. It would be the jewel of their India operations, providing thousands of jobs and delivering $1 billion in development aid to local communities.

But first POSCO needed to overcome a major hurdle: 50,000 people lived on the farmland that POSCO needed to make their plant a reality. As part of POSCO's agreement with Odisha, the local government offered to resettle the farmers in exchange for a hefty cash settlement from the company. But instead of buying them new farmland, officials forced them into barbed wire tent cities and pocketed the resettlement money. Concerned farmers tried to speak to POSCO, but keeping everything "by the book," POSCO refused, referring them back to the very officials who stole their resettlement funds. With a groundbreaking set to begin, POSCO highlighted the investment in 2010 as a "success story" of working with the local community.

After a year of begging government officials to be released, the displaced farmers grew desperate. They joined forces with criminal groups who attacked POSCO's offices and kidnapped visiting executives who came in to christen the site. One kidnapper delighted in telling us how they gave the shocked South Korean managers "a good thrashing" for their ignorance before dumping them at the nearest bus stop with orders to never return.

---

[34] The POSCO case as presented here is an abridged consolidation of Katsos and Miklian (2021) and Miklian (2012). Also see Miklian (2017).

After ten painful years and one billion lost dollars, POSCO abandoned its jewel without building a single permanent structure. POSCO wrote off the entire endeavor, claiming in 2015 that the project failed "because the Indian government has changed the law" and that they were a victim of unforeseeable circumstances.[35] Meanwhile, the displaced lived for a decade in POSCO-branded tent cities as local officials sold their annexed land to domestic industrial firms instead of giving it back.

What could POSCO have done differently?[36] An extra-legal approach would have carried a basket of positive outcomes. While following the law is important for avoiding legal issues, it does not provide a competitive advantage or drive profitability. In crisis settings, companies that exceed legal requirements to consider ethical practices through stakeholder needs tend to achieve long-term success. Incorporating ethics into board decision-making and corporate governance can enhance company performance on financial and nonfinancial measures, as can engaging in practices that align with local needs and values. Moreover, companies that solely focus on legal compliance may miss out on opportunities for innovation.

Our research showed that "best practice" can also splinter in polycrisis. For example, when POSCO, a company we'll examine more below, prioritized adherence to local laws and regulations, their operational and regulatory metrics sparkled. However, that very adherence sank the project because it did not take into account the local societal dynamics. A more holistic interpretation to best practice integrates the social, political, and operational issues to better understand the societal ramifications of operational acts. Had POSCO done this, perhaps they could have worked with government officials and local communities to ensure that local grievances were heard and helped resolve them as part of the community within which they operated.

Firms can have a temptation to obfuscate and confuse consumers and regulators to delay the reckoning of when the law will catch up with what society knows to be right. In 1903, Coca-Cola was one of a thousand forgettable upstarts in the new market of fizzy drinks. It also had enough cocaine in twenty-four ounces to equal one bump. But doctors knew that daily cocaine usage was not the healthiest habit and was enabling a nation of addicts.

While competitors trashed the findings and lobbied government to keep cocaine legal, Coca-Cola eliminated cocaine *before* regulators and social pressures forced them to. They switched to caffeine as their active ingredient, albeit at triple the concentration of today's version. That decision – seeing an

[35] POSCO 2015.
[36] Sources for this paragraph include: Yusuf et al., 2014; Yildiz et al., 2017; Lichtenthaler, 2019; Salin et al., 2019; Teixeira et al., 2021.

imminent sociopolitical shift and making a fundamental change to the business – is why Coca-Cola exists today, and why their cocaine-laced competitors like Vin de Coca de Perou, Liebig's Coca Beef Tonic, Dr. Sampson's Coca Spirits, Dope Cola, and Cola-Coca vanished into the historical ether.

What do the POSCO and Coca-Cola cases tell us? Two things. First, that making hard ethical decisions in crisis is something that nearly every firm faces at some point, but the guidance that currently exists for firms is not only woefully inadequate, following it can ruin the bottom line. In times of crisis, ethical leadership that uses legal guidelines as the primary framework for response decision-making risks prioritizing anti-society policies that do more harm to the firm than an ethics-first approach.

Second, these decisions are more consequential to the future of the firm than even many ethical business scholars realize. Just as the wrong decision can sink a large firm, the right decision by a small firm can send it soaring into the stratosphere. Ethics and strategy are interlinked concepts, and their complementarity is essential to recognize in crisis situations where their consequences are felt most strongly, in negative or positive directions.

Section Summary

We offer a quick recap of our main findings. First, **being lawful doesn't necessarily imply ethical – or profitable – behavior** under crisis. Evidence from POSCO in India and Firestone in India shows how adhering to the letter of the law enabled unethical (but presumably profitable) corporate behavior to take root. In crisis settings, this disconnect can trigger sociopolitical changes that carry significant negative impacts on the firm.

Second, **traditional best practice guidance can be ineffective or harmful in polycrisis settings**. This finding lies in the gap between what best practice aims to deliver and actual business roles in society. While this division has always carried a sense of false dichotomy, in crisis settings, this interrelation is at its most striking. Our research in seven fragile cities showed that firms that were the most effective at breaking these boundaries, and who eschewed internally-oriented "best practice" on what to do during a crisis, were more successful. Moreover, polycrisis carried a multiplier effect for these differences, suggesting that under these conditions, centering firm roles in society as the *most* important practice may have merit.

Third, while all firms aim to nurture trust with employees, consumers, and the public in crisis situations, this **trust cannot be bought or certified; it must be earned** through the hard work of building responsible sociopolitical relationships. While it is intuitive that authentic trust will resonate more than superficial gestures, our research showed that if a leader replaces superficial trust building with real, engaged effort, stakeholders reward the company.

These findings are integrative and overlapping. The Starbucks case shows how applying best practice trust markers superficially and prioritizing law over ethics had disastrous, yet preventable, consequences for the firm and its stakeholders. Starbucks arrived to Lake Toba with great intentions and a savior mentality. What Starbucks didn't investigate too closely was *why* the landowners hadn't shifted to other, more profitable crops earlier. They knew that the rubber mafia was present but assumed that farmers had more choice than they did in deciding what to plant and assumed that they could ignore the rubber cabal without incurring legal or reputational risks.

The rubber interests didn't turn tail just because Starbucks showed up. The rubber interests were also members of the community. When they weren't incorporated in Starbucks' plan, they reacted through political pressure, extortion, and violence. Starbucks thought them irrelevant to coffee. But bad actors don't just go away if they're ignored.

Learning how to discover the signal from sociopolitical noise in complex crisis situations is key to overcoming this challenge. Thus, our next Section provides evidence on how leaders can apply ethical precepts to survive through crisis by building a more holistic blueprint for the firm's sociopolitical role.

3 Partnerships and Building Resilience

Spilling the Tea: The Foundations of Leadership Success in Polycrisis

From 1983 to 2009, Sri Lanka's brutal civil war killed an estimated 50,000 people and led to massive population displacement within Sri Lanka and abroad. Driven by ethnic disputes primarily around the role of Tamil identity within Sri Lanka, violence and extortion of civilians and businesses were common, even outside of the centers of violence in the north and east.

Sri Lanka's primary export at the time was tea. The war drove many of the tea production companies out of business in the first decade or forced them to sell, but that was little consolation for many of the plantations and their workers. British and Australian-owned plantations had shut their doors or paid bribes from threats they had received. The rebels aimed to starve the government of foreign currency by stopping its major export, including threatening to poison the country's entire tea supply as it left the ports to foreign lands.

Near the start of the war, Merrill J. Fernando decided to start his own tea company. Fernando had trained with master tea tasters in England, which had used Fernando's home island – what was then called Ceylon – as the crux of its global, colonial tea growing and exporting operations. After independence, the newly named Sri Lanka was still beholden to massive tea companies that dominated the trade before independence.

What Fernando started and ran was a truly Sri Lankan tea company, one that would help retain earnings locally from Sri Lanka's main export, instead of reenacting the colonial dynamics through shareholder dividends paid to private companies in the UK and Australia. Within a decade, though, Sri Lanka was embroiled in the brutal civil war into which Fernando's tea company, Dilmah, was born.

One day during this time, Fernando recounted a story of a rumpled canvas bag sitting at the top step leading into Merrill Fernando's office trailer. From this ramshackle structure, Fernando ran Dilmah on a verdant and incessantly humid plantation. Fernando and his site manager crunched numbers inside while the chugging air conditioner pumped out a small river that flowed around the recently placed bag. Nobody saw how it got there.

Looking up from his ledger, Fernando saw the parcel and walked out to pick it up.

"Bananas?" his site manager guessed, shrugging his shoulders. Maybe a worker stashed a cool snack for later. Fernando shook his head, feeling the heavy content rolling around inside. A worker wouldn't rope a bag this tightly shut just for his treats.

"Coconuts," Merrill guessed, but he knew that wasn't quite right either. The bag weighed about too much for coconuts but the shapes inside seemed round. "Grab a machete."

Fernando brought the bag in while the manager ran to the toolshed. The blast of chill air gave Fernando flashbacks to England where he trained as a tea master.

In the tea industry, half a million so-called "Estate Tamils," tea plantation workers of Tamil ethnic identity distinct from those fighting in the north and east of the country, were the backbone of the tea workforce. Early in the war, most of Fernando's competitors went out of business from the conflict combined with a global economic slowdown. Fernando started Dilmah in the shadow of these fears in 1985, along with hundreds of employees and suppliers who depended upon the company.

Fernando dropped the bag on his desk on top of assorted receipts, longhand letters to vendors, and ledgers with far more red entries than black. The site manager rushed in and handed over a blade, rusted at the end, but good enough to crack open some coconuts. Fernando grabbed the top of the bag and slit it open while the manager's mouth watered.

The manager reached in and grabbed one. His smile turned to horror. He wasn't holding the rough light brown hair of a coconut, but instead the straight black hair of a human head. The manager jumped away, turning pale.

Fernando spread the bag open. Three heads with glassy eyes stared back, all young Sri Lankan men chopped unevenly just below the jaw. Fernando swallowed his fear, then looked closer, puzzled.

"Whose heads are these?" Fernando asked. The site manager took one look at them, then bolted to the door and threw up on the stairs. Fernando squinted at the lifeless faces in vain for clues. He rummaged into the bloody bag, finding a note. Fernando unfolded the scribbled paperwork:

SEND YOUR WORKERS HOME
OR MORE WILL DIE.

Fernando rubbed his temples. A British plantation one valley away shut its doors the previous month from a similar threat. Others had too earlier that year. He knew who was behind it: the Tamil Tigers, the rebel group fighting the government. Their goal was to intimidate tea producers to starve the government of foreign currency by stopping its major export – tea. Up to that point, the tactic had a 100 percent success rate.

But Fernando knew something that the Tigers hadn't counted on. He knew the faces of every one of his workers and their families. And he'd never seen these faces before – they were just some poor random kids killed for a scare tactic. It worked on the foreign or absentee owners; they saw workers as little more than an endless cog of interchangeable bodies. But Fernando's decade of working with the community gave him a key piece of information that could save his business.

With his manager still heaving on the watery steps, Fernando picked up the phone to ring up one of the world's deadliest rebel groups. Nobody would scare him out of his shack. And nobody was going to scare his hundreds of workers and their families out of a job. But in his recollection, the conversation wasn't angry; it was firm. Dilmah would keep operating its tea plantations, workers would continue to be paid, and the company would not give in to intimidation or extortion.

Fernando knew many of the rebels around his facilities and their families. He knew the police and military officers around his facilities. He was intimately connected to his local community even while running a massive agricultural, manufacturing, and marketing operation. And every one of those employees, rebels, and government soldiers knew something about Fernando and Dilmah Tea: Sri Lanka was their home, and they weren't going anywhere.

Fernando's solidarity with his fellow citizens seeped into every aspect of the company's culture. Dilmah had the social licenses and insurance to operate from the higher wages they paid their plantation workers to the better working conditions they experienced. And they were explicitly political, advocating for nonviolence. His company culture combined three key values: solidarity, fairness, and courage. Despite being a member of a religious minority, Fernando's oft-repeated phrase was, "We are all children of Sri Lanka." This meant not caving to pressure from rebel groups any more than it meant not caving to pressure from the government.

And it worked.

Dilmah Tea survived because of a company culture that focused on its workers, not its corporate health. This seems obvious in hindsight but at the time was revolutionary. Sri Lankan plantation workers had been mistreated for almost the entirety of the century of British control of the tea plantations. In a country ravaged by ethnic violence, Dilmah's position was radical.

Fernando faced repeated death threats. When they threatened his employees, Fernando did their work himself. He emboldened his employees, who then refused to be threatened themselves. Fernando's focus on preparing for constant crisis meant stockpiling cash instead of paying shareholders dividends. Dilmah could keep paying its workers and was the only operation not beset by worker strikes that crippled its competitors.

By the end of the civil war, Fernando had grown Dilmah to the world's sixth-largest tea brand. Fernando's community engagement and focus on solidarity, fairness, and courage provided stability for employees and customers who could depend on Dilmah to do the right thing – and depend on their paychecks. Dilmah succeeded because it held strong to values that focused on how the company could help address the root causes of the conflict. And the culture that Fernando built was not a culture *in* crisis, but a culture born *of* crisis. Fernando realized that treating crisis as a taboo topic only exacerbated the consequences, so he dove into the problem when he could at least partially dictate its terms. Leaders like Merrill Fernando who understand their sociopolitical context are more likely to survive in polycrisis.

In this Section, we explore questions like: *How do companies and their leaders obtain social acceptance through community engagement? Why does community engagement help companies survive crises? And, How can leaders use partnerships – including with competitors – to engage with their communities?* We show how community engagement includes cooperating with the community and even competitors on issues of critical importance to succeed.

First, we look at how community engagement is crucial for building resilience before a crisis, as it establishes a "social license to operate" and helps organizations anticipate and better respond to crises. Then we'll see how organizational culture plays a critical role in facilitating community engagement. Finally, we examine how and why companies can form alliances with competitors during crises, which can be the difference between survival and bankruptcy. These alliances not only help firms survive but also have a positive impact on peace.

Community Engagement and the Social License to Operate

Community engagement consists of the active participation and collaboration between enterprises and the communities in which they operate. It involves forming alliances, cultivating relationships, and communicating with community members to address social, economic, and environmental issues.[37] Effective community engagement requires business leaders to be dedicated to shaping the values, norms, and practices by valuing community partnerships, collaboration, and the community's well-being. Businesses can thus establish trust, enhance their reputation, and contribute to the sustainable development of the communities they serve. In short, community engagement is about earned legitimacy.

To see this in practice, we go to the jungles of central India to follow Ratan Tata's humbled footprints. Tata was CEO of the $85 billion Tata Group, one of India's largest conglomerates. Throughout the 2000s, Tata Group hosted essential extractive operations in Jharkhand in the middle of a civil war against a Maoist insurgency that left 15,000 dead. At first, Tata tried to insulate itself from the violence by building schools and hospitals, and delivering free health care, all what might be considered "traditional CSR." But those initiatives

---

[37] Sources for this paragraph include: Laschewski et al. (2002), Reay et al. (2015), Cho et al. (2016), Nikolova & Andersen (2017), and Landrum & Ohsowski (2018).

infuriated thousands who couldn't access the benefits because they were just outside the firm's operational zone. Crossing the line between the haves and have-nots was as clear as walking from one village to another. And many of those left out of the fruits of the economic development supported the Maoists to get revenge on a confused Tata, which found its facilities and even schools sabotaged by guerrillas.

Why did Tata bother to work in such a fraught environment? Two reasons: One, Tata leadership believed that the company was one of the "good guys" in the space; and, two, the company was under intense national pressure to expand. Until 2008, Tata burnished their "green" credentials by highlighting efficiency and job creation, and their corporate reputation was one of India's best. The Indian Government aimed to quadruple mining sector investment to $90 Billion by 2030, so they securitized extraction as not only essential to growth but also to build relationships with developed country powers as a reliable supplier. Tata's growth wasn't just a shareholder issue, but one of national security.

In India, raw material production and land acquisition are framed in language arguing that economic growth is for the good of the nation. However, this approach also made it harder for marginalized populations living in those same spaces to make nonviolent grievances for fear of being branded an enemy of the state. When some agitated for change, Tata felt caught in the middle, as legislation designed to protect the land rights of indigenous populations was trumped by trade concerns. Worse, their grievances were rooted in inequalities that Tata's extractive policies exacerbated. Tata needed to tackle sociopolitical issues like inequality and group grievances head-on if it was to avoid following POSCO's fate from Chapter 2.

With the government expecting Tata to fill in for their own failures in the frontier, Tata first tried to fix the symptoms of the anger. They built hospitals and schools, trying to fix the government's governance failures and lack of capacity. But Tata was shocked to learn that these expensive measures didn't make the community happy. Instead, they were even angrier, both at the government for not doing their duty to build these components themselves, and at Tata for trying to whitewash over the community's actual grievances.

Eventually, Tata learned a business-changing lesson: When you pretend to be the government, people will treat you like the government. Once Tata invested more deeply in social understanding of the causes and consequences of the conflict, they better directed their philanthropic largesse through building up local government capacities, like delivering a more effective, less corrupt justice system and increased access to grievance mechanisms. This reduced local tensions – and secured more profitable and more secure operations for the firm.

This is a counter-intuitive finding that we impress upon managers in crisis settings: Islands of corporate-financed peace and prosperity can be more conflict-inducing and reputation-damaging than doing nothing at all in a sea of poverty and conflict. It often surprises leaders who assume that doing *something* must be better than nothing. These activities often fall under the guise of "traditional" CSR and ESG activities. But traditional CSR programs may not effectively address community issues, and almost never deliver positive impacts for communities outside the "benefit zone," as we saw with Tata.

Moreover, if their primary function is as a marketing instrument to improve the image and reputation of a company, this prioritization can also damage a firm's reputation. Although CSR activities can have positive effects on stakeholders and society, they may not be comprehensive or long-term solutions to complex community problems, necessitating genuine engagement with stakeholders to meet community requirements.[38] Our research found that money was better spent on working actively with communities to jointly solve problems from scratch, rather than deploying standardized programs in very different operational contexts.

Community engagement helps companies gain knowledge that is inaccessible from behind a desk. Fernando at Dilmah Tea knew civil conflict was brewing because he walked among his community. This meant listening to employees, government, *and* rebel people too. Fernando embodied research showing how listening helps leaders anticipate crisis events, and how community engagement generates opportunities to stand out from competition.[39] Using community partnerships to their fullest requires a culture of integrative organizational leadership. Cross-sector partnerships, such as business-NGO partnerships, can have substantial effects, effectively leveraging community relationships. In sum, businesses benefit when they engage in a community and share valuable knowledge.

There are no shortcuts, however. The only sound path through the wilderness is to look and listen. This seems absurdly simple. Yet corner a CEO in a 5-star hotel lounge after their third martini, and they'll tell you why they ignore the advice: They're afraid that once they hear what local communities want, then they'll have to do it (or be legally required to take action), and that might adversely impact the bottom line. When managers visit, they take highly curated tours of facilities and rarely engage with people living in the communities in which they operate. They avoid hard conversations, perceiving them as an interference. Yet without talking to the local community, there's no way to know what's needed and survive the crisis around the corner.

---

[38] (Cole & Roberts, 2011; Chakraborty & Jha, 2019; Steenkamp & Rensburg, 2019).
[39] (Collier & Esteban, 2007; Schau et al., 2009; Gruss et al., 2020).

Competitors Are Your Secret Weapon against Politics

Sun rays bounced through the bullfighting ring's stained-glass roof, painting a kaleidoscope of yellows, oranges, and reds across Luis Moreno's proud face.[40] Here in the mountain town of Tovar, Venezuela, the Corrida de Toros was the year's top social and sporting event rolled into one, a Kentucky Derby of the Andes. Moreno closed his eyes in gratitude, letting the warmth bathe his beefy cheeks.

Today was as fine a day as any to go bankrupt.

As spectators filtered in, rifling through their programs and chatting about which bull might defy insurmountable odds to survive the day, Moreno and his new wife shared a pained smile. Moreno became a pillar of Tovar's business community by building the valley's best motorcycle repair shop, two decades of grimy work tearing apart and rebuilding Harleys and Hondas. And Moreno was a fighter too, scrapping with biker gangs to collect payment when he had to. They were dressed to kill, just like the matador that entered the ring.

But underneath the grandeur, not all was as it appeared. Moreno's suit frayed at the cuffs. His wife's earrings were zirconia. Their *pamperos*, leather canteens, were filled with third-rate rum more suitable to run his pickup, not the usual top shelf Diplomatico or even the quite acceptable Cacique.

Hard times or not, today called for celebration. Moreno even gave his mom a wave and tipped his black hat from one section over. Mama Moreno, flanked by Moreno's dad and ex-wife, shot daggers back to her only son. She wasn't mad about Moreno's new arm candy. What really burned her up had its origins a couple of years back. Toxic politics had infected the Moreno family like a virus, as it had countless families across Venezuela.

When a bombastic politician named Hugo Chavez took over Venezuela in 1999, he promised a return to the good old days by draining the corrupt Caracas swamp. Chavez said he alone could fix Venezuela's problems. At campaign events, he ranted incessantly that anyone who tried to stop him, or even disagreed with him, was a hater, a loser, and a traitor. Chavez's rhetoric polarized society. Now people defined themselves not by where they came from or what they did, but if they were pro- or anti-*Chavista*.

Pro-Chavez Mama Moreno was sure that her candidate could cleanse Venezuela of its evil. Anti-Chavez Luis Moreno loathed the populist Chavez for his virulent attacks on capitalism. Mother and son had barely spoken in a year, each adamant that the other's political leaders would ruin the country.

Moreno ached over losing his mom to a slick savior ideology, but the polarization did more than fracture his family. Living in a pro-*Chavista* part

---

[40] Pseudonym used for protection, and some non-essential details have been changed to ensure security. Sources from this Section are author interviews and fieldwork.

of the country, loyal customers slipped through his fingers every week, instead of purchasing from *Chavista* dealerships. His ironclad rule of no politics at the shop helped a bit, but everyone knew his real beliefs.

And now, at the corrida de toros, politics had even infiltrated Moreno's safe space. A group of young men entered the grandstand, wearing all red and chanting slogans about the annexation of the profit hogs. Most in the crowd ignored them; nobody's opinions could be swayed anymore.

Chavistas. Moreno scowled. Not only had they warped his mother's critical thinking abilities, but under their rule, Venezuela's economy would be as doomed as the massive black bull behind the wooden gate. They quieted down as the gate burst open – even the *Chavistas* were smart enough to know when to let the games begin.

After a few minutes of pretending this was a fair fight, the crowd roared as the furious bull charged at the waving cape. The matador sidestepped the charge and stuck a flag in true at the back of the skull. Blood spurted out of the bull's body as it writhed. The matador preened.

Moreno took a swig of cheap rum, mesmerized by the bright red liquid streaming down the bull's heaving ribs. Wounded and outmatched, the bull foundered. The matador unsheathed his sword. Within minutes the bull would be dead. Within hours it would be served as spiced shredded beef to a few hundred people.

He looked over at the *Chavistas*, scowling as they cheered and laughed. The old fighter inside needed to take a stand before his own lifeblood drained to nothing. Desperation drove him to an audacious idea.

Moreno marched over, fists clenched. The *Chavistas* looked him up and down. Moreno returned the stare, like two heavyweights at a weigh-in. After an eternity, Moreno spoke.

"Caballeros, comrades. Let's do some business."

Moreno's ingenious realization was that by working alone, his business would die just as surely as the bull. But by working with his community in a time of crisis, by listening to their needs while being honest about his beliefs, and by building a bridge to his enemies, he not only saved his business – but grew it three times over.

Moreno's eureka moment unlocked his secret to success. Now, he owns one of the few firms that happily does business with both sides. Even his new business partner is a *Chavista*, and his company enjoys booming sales in a land torn apart by economic crisis and polarization.

The intense polarization in Venezuelan society had ripped the fabric of communities, turning towns like Tovar into microcosms of the strife that engulfed the whole country. After his conversation with those who'd once seemed implacable foes, Moreno seized a moment that translated to an enlightenment for his business endeavors. Businesses couldn't cast aside the churning political tides; they now had to navigate the thrashing waters with an adept hand.

Moreno led his repair shop to be an exemplar of communal cohesion, a business that transcended the societal divide that had so starkly colored Venezuelan streets maroon with dissatisfaction and betrayal. He understood that in the crux of conflict, the value of a business lay not just in the service or product it provided, but in the bridges it could build among its customers. His shop became a neutral ground – an oasis where those of any political hue could speak the universal language of motorcycle engines and chrome.

Moreno's nuanced approach was one of balanced pragmatism; his business did not become a platform for political diatribes but of professionalism and impartial service. His repair shop supported the entire community, including training programs for young mechanics, which cemented its position as an indispensable local enterprise. It became a sanctuary for discourse, catalyzing conversations that led to local initiatives aiming at economic resuscitation.

Moreno's actions also highlight the need for businesses to foster inclusion and mutual respect amidst a climate of divisiveness. Business leaders like Moreno, who actively pivot their operations to serve their communities, find their businesses not just surviving but thriving. But his actions also show the inevitable failure of these businesses to solve every polycrisis, however hard they might try to counter the fatalism that envelopes debates over how far companies should go in trying to address root causes of crises.

As Moreno discovered, one salve for business woes in turbulent times lies in transcending traditional roles – mediator, educator, and even peacemaker. Businesses that embed themselves in the fabric of their communities, advocate for unity instead of division, and practice inclusivity can become more than a mere business. They can become beacons of hope in tumultuous and divisive landscapes. Thus, we shine a light on the transformative power of business in bridging societal divides and fostering sustainable prosperity against all odds.

Community Engagement

Competitors are an often-forgotten part of the community. But allying with them and the community together when crisis strikes can have stronger benefits still. To see how this works in practice, we go to Cyprus, a favorite of European tourists for its beautiful beaches, Christian pilgrims for its monasteries and tombs (including the final resting of place of Lazarus), of Russian oligarchs who love its European Union ties and Cayman Islands-level banking secrets, and Middle Eastern traders who use it to access Europe. Cyprus was designed by its policymakers as a businessperson's paradise.

Cyprus is also home to one of the UN's longest serving peacekeeping missions. UN forces help keep the island's Turkish-speaking north separate from the Greek-speaking south. The international community and the EU recognize only the south as legitimate, while regional economic power – and erstwhile EU member candidate – Turkey recognizes the north alone, which is unsurprising given that Turkey's invasion led to the north's creation.

For decades, Cypriot businesses on both sides of the divide watched squabbling politicians fail to bring peace. In 2004, the politicians tried again, this time with a bigger prize in sight: If they could reconcile, the whole island could join the European Union. As talks kicked up the dust of broken promises from the past, companies of both north and south had an idea: They banded together to make a deal known as the Green Line Agreement. This should have been illegal cross-border collaboration. But there was a little-known loophole that the 2004 peace talks had brought out into the open: If an organization was established before 1968, it retained it's legal status on both sides of the divide. The Cypriot Chamber of Commerce and the Turkish Cypriot Chamber of Commerce both predated 1968.

Together, they conceived the first way to transport goods across the Green Line, the demilitarized zone managed by the UN peacekeepers. The Green Line Agreement became one of the few reconciliation measures to pass on both sides. Because of its success, Cyprus is a member of the European Union and the conflict, while still frozen, has become more of a nuisance than a business-killer with no violence in the twenty years since its passage.

Business partnerships of all types play a crucial role in helping businesses survive crises by contributing to their resilience and sustainability.[41] For example, collaborations with NGOs and community organizations offer businesses access to local knowledge, capabilities, and networks, and embeddedness within informal networks. By leveraging this expertise and resources, businesses make more informed decisions and respond effectively. Second, partnerships with community organizations enhance a business's reputation and legitimacy. Engaging in socially responsible initiatives and working closely with organizations that have a positive social impact can enhance a company's image and build trust with stakeholders. This can be particularly valuable during a crisis when businesses face increased scrutiny and need to demonstrate their commitment to social concerns. By forming strategic alliances with these organizations, businesses can strengthen their resilience and increase their chances of thriving in polycrisis.

---

[41] Sources for this paragraph include Webb et al. (2009), Eid & Sabella (2014), Nahi (2018), and Poret (2019).

Section Summary

The lessons that Dilmah Tea learned while surviving the impacts of the Sri Lankan Civil War were used again in response to the 2008 tsunami. They leveraged their prior experience with crisis management to reorganize their disrupted supply chain, support displaced farmers, customers, and their families, and help local communities rebuild. Their proactive disaster mitigation strategies, learned in the crucible of war, were instrumental in mitigating financial losses and maintaining continuity. Moreover, their ethical practices and emphasis on social responsibility united a workforce and customer base in their commitment to Dilmah, further exemplifying the resilience of this tea company amidst desperate conditions.

The first is to **move past conventional CSR activities**. A social license to operate unlocks the secret to risk reduction and gives a backbone for support during societal hardship. With it, factories keep humming, employees stay working, and businesses find protection from unlikely sources. Be it armed conflict or social conflict, when communities experience polycrisis, empty promises or philanthropy help no one. Tata discovered that communities quickly see through these activities as nonmeaningful. Successful businesses construct enduring programs rather than one-offs, and prove that they are in community "for the long haul," without fear that they would pack up and leave in the face of crisis, violence, or other difficulty.

Second, **educating managers is crucial to doing community engagement right** for gaining community acceptance and becoming a meaningful part of the community. Whether managers realize it or not, they impact the communities in which they operate. But locals can tacitly or explicitly revoke a company's social license to operate. We saw this when Tata was plagued by a Maoist insurgency. It can take decades to regain a lapsed license. Proactive managers emphasize that community welfare is a competitive advantage and prioritize engagement as an integral part of their duties. After all, management by walking around ("MBWA") only works when it is focused on active problem solving and is part of the manager's job.[42]

Our research indicates that companies that integrate themselves into a community gain legitimacy and reputational advantages over rivals, particularly where citizens have been persecuted. Managers are the "tip of the spear" here by personally interacting with communities. Fernando networked amongst his employees, the military, police, rebels, and their families and friends. This built personal trust and context-specific knowledge, which is indispensable when addressing complex hazards. If managers build local networks, they can

---

[42] (Tucker & Singer, 2015).

decipher the actual severity of prospective crises, and rumblings on the ground regarding impending threats.

Third, these strategies **can only be effective if a company's culture allows them to be used**. Leaders have a crucial role to play in creating organizational culture at every level.[43] For a multinational firm, leadership at the global, regional, unit, and factory levels *each* needs to promote a coherent company culture that allows for community engagement in disparate environments. Fernando did this by founding his company with values that were deeply held and deeply rooted within the communities Dilmah operated in. Companies without such a founding will have to work extremely hard in shaping a culture that allows for deep community engagement to gain community acceptance, while also standardizing practices in line with global and/or regional company values and legal regimes.

Finally, **businesses must invest in and cultivate community trust**. Relationships founded on trust can generate strong social connections that integrate the business into the fabric of the community, providing businesses with a difficult-to-replicate source of competitive advantage. Building localized knowledge starts by listening to local actors without preconceived assumptions about what they require, and comprehending their skills and competencies in addition to the political and social dangers they confront. Any leader wishing to cultivate trust and support in such environments must demonstrate – not simply assert – that it will be a committed partner in the community's survival.

---

[43] (Bass & Avolio, 1993; Schein, 2010).

4 Action Beyond Governments and Taking Principled Stands

I'd Like to Sell the World a Coke

In 1993, the same month that Yitzhak Rabin and Yasser Arafat inked their signatures onto the Oslo Peace Accords to bring peace to Israel and Palestine, Zaki Khouri, a Palestinian-American living in Florida, and his partners signed a deal with Coca-Cola to open a bottling plant in what would be the new Palestinian Territories. During the 1948 nakba, Khouri had fled his home and became a refugee, along with 700,000 other Palestinians. Brilliant and determined, he excelled in school and worked his way up the investment banking ladder in New York and London. When rumblings of a peace agreement started, Khouri decided to move back to Palestine aka the West Bank. He was one of many businesspeople who saw a huge opportunity for a newly opened market and the chance to rebuild a homeland he had never forgotten.

Finally, every Palestinian could get their first taste of Americana for themselves. But there was just one problem: Coca-Cola, a staunch supporter of Israel for forty years, was seen by Palestinians as nothing less than the devil's drink. Gaza was Pepsi land. Pepsi had operated bottling facilities there since 1961. Khouri's business plan received another blow when a right-wing Israeli group assassinated Rabin. His successor Benjamin Netanyahu largely abandoned the deal, leading to the first intifada, a violent rebellion by Palestinians against Israeli control.

In 1998, Khouri finally began to build his factory. But now there were new problems, specifically embargoes made it impossible to get machinery parts across the border. Khouri swallowed hard. Hat in hand, he asked Coca-Cola Israel for help. They agreed, but Khouri was certain his fellow Palestinians would consider working with Coca-Cola to be treasonous. Nevertheless, he talked openly about his intentions. Much like Merrill Fernando, he realized that transparency could be a secret weapon to continuity. He ensured that NBC – Khouri's new company – would always have a reliable supplier.

Most thought that engaging with both sides of the conflict was a suicidal choice, but to Khouri it was the only choice. In Israel, Coca-Cola global and its Israeli bottling company could push for the parts needed to get through the Israeli-controlled border with Gaza and the West Bank. Khouri could get materials across the Palestinian-controlled portion of the border by working with family and friends – his and his employees – to explain the importance of each component. They got the factory built.

Khouri took a similar approach to marketing. As a global giant, Coca-Cola could outspend pretty much anyone in advertising and marketing campaigns. But Palestinians would never accept generic messaging. So Khouri became the public face of Coca-Cola in Palestine, determined with every visible gulp to shed the drink's association with Israel.

The final challenge was the hardest: providing safe and reliable employment. With supply disruptions and violence, most companies shuttered for weeks at a time every year. When they reopened, some employees would invariably be wounded, dead, or imprisoned. NBC took a different approach. It opened for business every day, regardless of the violence or supply disruptions, even if shipments didn't arrive and there was nothing for workers to do. Providing consistency in a notoriously inconsistent place became its hallmark.

He also paid employees on time. Most disrupted companies wouldn't pay their employees for lost time, a perfectly sensible strategy. But NBC refused to stop the checks under one caveat – NBC and its warehouses were no-go zones for violence or the storage of any non-company items. It was a corporate green zone, a safe place accepted by all sides, only because of NBC's longstanding community commitment.

NBC became Palestine's most consistent economic actor, its third-largest employer, and fifth-largest private investor, turning Coca-Cola's reputation around. Shipments got through, and the Israelis trusted their contents. Khouri's culture was tailor-made for the community: stability, consistency, and nonviolence. NBC employees stayed out of the worst troubles. Consumers learned they could rely on a local company to produce Coca-Cola while other items more heavily subject to the blockade couldn't. And employees could rely on their paychecks every month regardless of what crisis might envelop their streets or their homes.

Khouri hasn't softened his ardent anti-occupation stance. He was a vocal supporter of the Boycott, Divest, and Sell (BDS) even after it became illegal in Israel. While Coca-Cola was sued and threatened to be forced to break ties, Khouri's reputation among Coca-Cola executives, Palestinians, and Israelis alike earned him support in spite of their disagreement with his position. NBC became a key part of Coca-Cola's ability to fend off BDS-related marketing pushes in other countries, especially in Malaysia.

In a polycrisis world, the days of companies "staying out of politics" are over. Companies that believe they can remain aloof from contentious issues are making their jobs harder. We have seen that impartiality to two or more sides is possible (and in some cases preferable), but neutrality is not a viable strategy. Customers view inaction as a sign of cowardice and judge such businesses negatively. Yet, inaction can also have dire consequences. Firms that take a position early, clearly, and in accordance with their values (rather than simply saying what they think their customers or shareholders want to hear) can develop new markets while minimizing losses from groups with which they disagree. In conflict contexts such as the Palestinian Territories, companies willing to make public, principled choices earned significant business from customers who disagreed with their positions, allowing them to outperform their apolitical competitors.

But working in accordance with company values can often mean having to go beyond basic legal and regulatory requirements. Companies must collaborate not only with, but also beyond, government agencies and officeholders. According to our research, the most common error businesses make is assuming that local appointed or elected officials are synonymous with community interests.[44] When public institutions are insufficient or obstructing progress, following the law alone is a prescription for disaster as we saw in Chapter 2.

Leaders must not be afraid to take principled political stands, and firms thrive when they work not just with, but also beyond, government agencies and officeholders. In our research, businesses partnering only with officials as if they are synonymous with community interests failed when institutions themselves were part of the crisis problem. Here we examine: *What does it mean for a company to take a principled stand? Why does going beyond government help companies survive in polycrisis? How can community engagement used to help companies pursue their values?*

We start by establishing why corporate principles are worth standing up for. This involves disentangling corporate speak and promotional material about "Values" to examine what the company actually supports through its policies and culture. We then show how taking principled stands requires companies to go beyond government guidance. Next, we look at how acting on authentic principles can help companies weather even the most complex and volatile crises.

Taking Authentic, Principled Stands

In translating our empirical work to leadership practice, we engage with some of the longstanding puzzles for organizational ethics scholars: How does a group establish and enact its values? Which members of the group have the most influence or should have the final say in what values the group will promote as its own? What can be done about tensions between individual member values and the values of the organization? It is not our goal to answer these questions, which are better suited to ethicists much smarter than ourselves. Rather, we examine what we have seen work for organizations and leaders in highly politicized contexts. First, we show what they have done that worked; then we will show how those examples connect to our research and that of others.

---

[44] For example, Miklian (2012) and Katsos (2019).

There are few issues weighing quite so heavily on the minds of American business leaders more than the politicization of everything in society today, where someone gets furious at seemingly every decision or nondecision they take. The common prescription would be to avoid political confrontation wherever possible and try to weather the storm. After all, everything is politicized today, and we can't escape it, right? Our research suggests that such advice is wrong. It's not increased politicization that's driving a wedge between business and customers; it's increased *polarization*, worse now than at any time since 1865. To wit, 50 percent of Americans boycotted a company in the last five years alone. How can anyone work with both sides? Chobani and Chick-Fil-A can provide some clues.

Hamdi Ulukaya, a Kurdish refugee who fled horrific violence and persecution in Iraq and immigrated to the United States, was little more than a victim at first. America was Hamdi's promised land. He found happiness in his adopted home. But there was just one problem – America's yogurt was awful! Ulukaya pined for a childhood he could never revisit due to the war, a youth of feta making and heavenly fresh yogurt.

Living in upstate New York, he found remnants of the Rust Belt's decline – rich land and shuttered dairy farms. So in 2002, he started his own company in an abandoned facility to deliver dairy luxury to American palettes (and his own), one plastic cup at a time. He called it "shepherd" in Kurdish. The translation? Chobani.

Chobani's Kurdish connection didn't stop with the name. Ulukaya hired refugees who had fled to the US, just like he had. He funded projects for undernourished kids, just like he had been. He helped communities where his factories operated so that they wouldn't leave misery in their wake if they closed. Then Ulukaya hired lobbyists to push for these same policies nation-wide. He filled 30 percent of his workforce with refugees and gave away 10 percent of his shares to employees.

When Donald Trump came into the Oval Office in 2017 with an anti-refugee and nativist platform, Chobani's political environment was upended. Online trolls attacked Chobani mercilessly, leading national boycotts by arguing that he wanted "to drown the United States in Muslims," all because he dared give refugees a job. But Ulukaya hired even *more* refugees. The boycotts were quickly dwarfed by counter-boycotts. Chobani's sales skyrocketed.

It can be easy to think that companies that have a more progressive stance are more likely to survive crisis and uncertainty. To be clear, that is *not* what our research has shown. We have seen believers in every side to a conflict figure out the same lesson: that neutrality is not an option and values must be authentic and openly communicated. To drive that lesson home, let's look at a company in the US from the opposite side of the political spectrum.

In 1946, S. Truett Cathy, a Christian from the southeastern US, founded his fast-food chain, Chick-fil-A. In his words, he "based his business on Biblical principles that he believed were also good business principles . . . to glorify God by being a faithful steward of all that is entrusted to us." His business contributes to charities that fight same-sex marriage and promote abstinence-only sex education. The Human Rights Campaign Buyer's Guide – a leading LGBTQ+ NGO – rated the company a perfect Zero.

Fast-food jobs in America are not considered great employment. Yet at Chick-fil-A, workers make above minimum wage, get regular time off including the famous mandatory Sunday closures of all restaurants, and earn profit-sharing, 401k's, and full medical and dental coverage. Chick-fil-A franchises are highly sought after because they produce more revenue per store than any other fast food chain in America, yet they are also inexpensive to obtain with the process for franchisees focused on the values, fit, and work ethic rather than how much wealth they have already accumulated. The franchising of Chick-fil-A hasn't made the rich richer as with other franchises; it rather has been a boon to hard-working middle-class Americans to have opportunities for advancement. Their highest paid executive makes $700,000 per year.

Chick-fil-A's public politics have dragged them more than once into culture war storms. Yet its sales have tripled during that same time while other fast-food outlets have seen theirs fall due to economic and industry shifts. Chick-fil-A also crafted and implemented a culture of values throughout its operations, particularly in employee treatment. Chick-fil-A became a lightning rod for a culture war, but in the actual definition of the term. They took the damaging strikes at the very top of their headquarters from the CEO on down; let them flow through the firm's solid infrastructure by saying that they respect others' positions but won't change theirs; insulating their brand time and again.

Chick-fil-A executives took to heart that customers will only respect your values if they respect your product. To wit, Pete Buttigieg, gay 2020 Democratic candidate for President said, "I do not approve of their politics. I kind of approve of their chicken." Be it a company or an individual, one must deliver clear, sustained community value if one expects that community to respect values it does not agree with in Chick-fil-A's case both in how it treats its workers and in what those workers dish up to the community.

Both Chick-fil-A and Chobani show that company's values are not as important as appearing to be *authentic*. "Christian values" for Chick-fil-A means treating workers with respect as fellow creations of God and a deep commitment to the service of others, just as it means not supporting LGBTQ+ causes. Ulukaya's Chobani supports refugee employment even as it uses lobbying to help promote it. For both companies, their values are their values regardless of whether they are politically convenient or good marketing. That makes their values something that critics can attack, but they also make clear to allies and enemies alike that they are open for business to everyone, regardless of whether their customers agree with them.

This distinction is the core of being "impartial" towards customers, but not "neutral." Both companies want to produce their best product within the boundaries of their values. Those values were linked to the morals of their founders, and, in Chick-fil-A's case, have been continued by their successors. Both companies have also remained private, which may be key to maintaining a more values-driven culture.[45]

Neutrality and impartiality have distinct meanings. Neutrality refers to a state of being outside of politics, providing goods or services to all individuals and shielding employees from political demands. However, claims to neutrality are often deconstructed, as the provision of goods and services cannot be entirely divorced from their impacts. Impartiality refers to the fair and unbiased treatment of individuals, regardless of their affiliations or circumstances. In crisis zones, impartiality is crucial because it recognizes the impossibility of neutrality (everyone has a bias) while also recognizing the business imperative of self-interest (we'll do business with anyone). While neutrality aims to create a space disconnected from politics, impartiality ensures fairness in business. Taking principled stands means showing your bias, and letting everyone know that you're open for business anyway.

Companies avoid politics because they worry about alienating customers, suppliers, and governments. But trying to be above politics or pretending to have no opinion doesn't minimize such risks. It only makes the business a scapegoat. If a business does not stand up for the side it agrees with, that side will have no incentive to support it in times of need. And if it doesn't stand against the side it doesn't agree with, people will assume that it stands with them. It's unrealistic for firms to avoid politics because everyone, including the company and the people who make a company, are already enmeshed in society, especially in polarized environments.

Going Beyond Government Guidance

An authentic firm that wishes to survive in crisis must conquer this significant challenge: It must never trust the government alone when it says a policy is "good enough" for a community. Let's return to Coca-Cola in Palestine. Against a backdrop of clashing political ideologies, import restrictions, and a volatile security landscape, Khouri adopted an approach that was bold yet balanced. He

---

[45] (Deephouse, 2013; Orr et al., 2014; Panwar et al., 2014).

stopped adhering to governmental guidance calling for heightened security checks for products crossing the border. Instead, Khouri strategically partnered with the Israeli bottling company and local community networks in Palestine to facilitate the passage of necessary components.

This approach went over and above (and sometimes legally around) what the government mandated as they utilized relationships, not official routes, to navigate the complex political landscape. During periods of heightened tensions, Khouri ensured smooth operations by weaving a corporate culture of stability, consistency, and nonviolence, creating a bubble of normalcy in an otherwise turbulent environment. He did not merely stick to governmental guidelines but surpassed them in his pursuit of community development by interpreting guidelines as a starting point. Khouri's venture was firmly rooted in the belief that this was not just about selling a drink, but pitching a symbol of stability, of normality, and of hope against the backdrop of turmoil and distress.

Being transparent, honest, and active in social issues earns respect from customers, even if they disagree with you.[46] When you are transparent and authentic, you will find seemingly odd bedfellows for a common and mutually rewarding future. Competitors and enemies can also be allies in times of uncertainty. The values that Khouri created in NBC corporate culture were quite different from those that Fernando imbued in Dilmah. And that's exactly the point: What the community needs is different in every situation.

Yet the crisis in both settings was the basis for their organizational cultures. Different root causes of crisis will require different crisis-proof cultures. And values must address the root causes of the conflict. Like Fernando, Khouri paired this culture with an open political role and social license to operate. Khouri's statements against the Israeli occupation were rooted in stability, consistency, and nonviolence, but that didn't stop him from criticizing others for their use of violence. And his point was consistent: There was unacceptable violence on both sides, but it was not equal. More Palestinians died than Israelis. Palestinians were not stopping necessary goods; it was a one-way blockade. Yet that never excused terrorist attacks. This stance earned Khouri the role as a trusted voice even among Israelis.

Community Engagement Requires Time

Importantly, moving beyond government guidance requirement time engaged with the community, and it's never too late for a business to regain community trust. The Federación Nacional de Cafeteros de Colombia (FNC), founded in

---

[46] Sources for this paragraph include: Frynas (2010), Hansen & Flyverbom (2015), Crick & Crick (2020), Halan & Signh (2023).

1927 and popularly known as Juan Valdez, learned this lesson just in time.[47] The FNC is one of Colombia's largest and most important businesses, a public and private alliance of 500,000 coffee producers. Historically it prioritized strong relationships with its farmers, but as the company grew and became a conglomerate in the 1990s, the importance of this connection lost priority.

But by 2008, amid the global financial crisis, coffee prices were crashing, FNC was losing money quarter after quarter, and long-simmering conflicts between the government and insurgents reignited into war. Luis Genaro Muñoz, the CEO of FNC, received a stream of reports that grew worse by the day: destroyed supply lines, extorted farmers, and executions of staff by guerrillas and paramilitaries. Farmers no longer saw FNC as a trusted voice they could rely upon, and began to abandon their farms. Muñoz cycled through standard fixes of increased protection and supply chain management to no avail, and felt pressure to ride out the conflict by cutting costs and securing FNC's assets, standard "best practice" advice.

But standard crisis management fixes – including pulling out of the worst-hit areas – were the exact things that would endanger FNC's local employees. They would also harm the company's long-standing business model, which depended on small-scale Colombian coffee producers; in fact, FNC's product was marketed around them. Muñoz realized that he needed a new model. With his company's future on the line, Muñoz took three radical steps.

First, he made the company the public face of peacebuilding in the coffee regions. This meant putting FNC branding on peace initiatives that had no guarantee of success and using the company's political capital to bring key actors to the negotiation table, building trust in FNC amongst communities that had given up hope that FNC cared about their security situation. If it worked, the government, rebels, and local community could all rebuild society together with help from FNC. If it failed, he'd take the blame for a failed peace and a new spiral of violence.

Second, Muñoz transformed FNC's relationship with its farmers from one of buyer and occasional benefactor to one of partners in crisis. Working with the United Nations, the Spanish Agency for International Development Cooperation, and the NGO *Humanismo y Democracia*, Muñoz integrated national and international development agencies into his company's operations in hundreds of villages, building long-term projects aimed at finding solutions that worked for all stakeholders, even FARC and the paramilitaries.

---

[47] The Juan Valdez case as presented here is an abridged consolidation of Miklian & Medina Bickel (2020) and Miklian et al. (2021).

These weren't simplistic CSR-style initiatives like donating money or supplies; they were in-depth consultations that treated the business, the local community, and authorities as equal participants, with equal stakes in their mutual success. Over painful months, the community trust returned. Muñoz hired 1,000 people across the country to distribute peacebuilding training modules at village roundtables, train their neighbors and fellow citizens in community engagement and dialogue, and facilitate farming and sustainability best practices.

Third, and most audacious of all, Muñoz invited both the leftist guerrillas and the rightest paramilitaries to the village roundtables, knowing that, without their buy-in, any cease-fire would be impossible. By uniting everyone, and finding new ways to go forward together, Muñoz aimed to build a profitable local peace in FNC's operational areas, one that would be stronger than what even the Colombian government's own initiatives could achieve.

The roundtables started tenuously; most local communities refused to sign on out of skepticism or fear, and insecurity grew as insurgents and paramilitaries warned the farmers against organizing. Muñoz persisted, publicly committing to double the project's length to a decade and making a multiyear financial commitment to ensure that peacebuilding activities would be completed.

In total, 10,000 brave coffee farmers responded to Munoz by doing something radical of their own: They banded together, hoping that there would be strength in numbers. Some were murdered as a result, but that didn't stop the rest. They used their collective strength to tackle the conflict head-on, holding community dialogues and peacebuilding trainings under the threat of death. Eventually, FARC commanders and paramilitary members joined the initiative, seeing more to gain from a transition to peace than from yet another cycle of war. Confident that FNC was a trusted broker that wouldn't vanish this time if violence spiked, farmers began to rebuild their communities. By uniting everyone with the most to lose from war (including themselves), and finding new ways to go forward together, Juan Valdez built a profitable peace stronger than even the Colombian government's own peace agreements achieved.

After one year, the security situation improved so much that FNC farmers could return to their fields. They regained trust in their employer and have returned that favor through increased loyalty and corporate support even during lean price years. FNC not only survived in one of the world's most dangerous crisis zones but expanded its coffee sales into thirty-two countries. Its farmers earn higher prices and have greater yields all while living and working in a safer, more secure, and more sustainable business environment.

Multilevel and reciprocal trust building can establish a foundation of credibility, reliability, and integrity, which is essential for sustainable value creation when engaging with vulnerable communities.[48] Trust can be fostered by adhering to stated principles and ethical norms, and through reliable behavior, good communication, and goal-congruence. Trust is also closely linked to organizational identification, where employees develop a sense of belonging and commitment, and a firm that is perceived as trustworthy and ethically responsible is more likely to attract and retain customers, investors, and partners. Small businesses in particular benefit from community-based networks and social capital, and being proactive in creating partnerships makes them more likely to thrive during crises.

But sometimes, all of the above still isn't enough, and a leader needs to make an exceptional leap of faith.

Putting in the Work for Peace

Shaking his head, Michael Young pulled off his horn-rimmed spectacles on a dreary November 1987 afternoon. The nondescript career civil servant pinched the bridge of his nose, wishing he was anywhere other than this dark bricked-up cellar about an hour west of London. In front of him sat two groups that saw the other as evil incarnate. If Young couldn't get them to agree, he'd be fired and blackballed from a job anywhere in the United Kingdom. Worse, the $5 billion company he worked for would be ruined. Worse yet, a country's best chance in a generation to find peace would be lost.

On one side of the conference table were multi-generation farmers, immensely powerful but naive about the ways of the world. On the other, a sophisticated besuited group looking to do some business. With everyone stuffed in this small-windowed basement, it seemed only a matter of time before tempers boiled over into yelling, if not a fistfight. After four hours, the only thing they agreed on was ordering the roast for lunch.

Young adjusted his already-impeccable bow tie and glanced out a little window, spying the neo-Gothic mansion that George Harrison bought when he quit the Beatles. Maybe he thought all the room needed was love, love, love.

As public affairs director for mining company Consolidated Gold Fields, Young played secret mediator between the South African apartheid government (the farmers) and the African National Congress (the suits). Gold Fields poached Young from the Prime Minister's office as the world hammered South Africa for its racist apartheid policy. Companies like Gold Fields were caught in the crossfire. Gold Fields needed a ringer who knew both business and politics

---

[48] Sources for this paragraph include: (Lumpkin & Dess, 1996; Surie & Ashley, 2007; Sundaramurthy, 2008; Ajmal et al., 2017; Rim & Dong, 2018; Srivastava et al., 2020; Belitski et al., 2021).

to keep them above the fray and beat back competitors attempting endless hostile takeovers.

Enter Young. He knew that if South Africa continued to spiral into chaos, international pariah-hood, and violence, there'd be no company left to save. So Young thought bigger. He drew up an insane idea to save not only Gold Fields but also all of South Africa: to end apartheid altogether. He convinced leaders of both groups to come to Henley-on-Thames to hash out their differences, a quiet little hamlet far removed from the global media circus.

Young realized his mistake immediately: How can one strike a deal between two groups of people when one didn't even see the other as fully human? He wrapped the meeting with a promise to himself that the next time they met, he'd be armed with every bit of information he could gather from the community on how to get the government and ANC to find common ground. Luckily for Young, both sides agreed to try again too.

After two years of high-stakes negotiations across England and South Africa, Young achieved the unthinkable. Along with the help of many others, Young brokered a peace deal between the ANC and the government, ending the apartheid regime in perhaps the greatest display of diplomacy by business in history. Young and Gold Fields were heroes.

Gold Fields reaped the benefits in weeks. The hostile takeover vultures morphed into eager investors. Profits and growth exploded. Within four years, Gold Fields became one of the world's biggest gold companies. By helping to generate a "good shock" – a rapid, fundamental societal change that dramatically improves human rights, civil liberties, or other bedrocks of egalitarian democracy – Young wasn't just a corporate icon, but an actual hero for the people of South Africa.

Young's biggest insight, one that he didn't realize himself at first, was that the best way to succeed is to be a part of making the change happen in the first place. It's an insight we've witnessed in firms big and small. One needn't broker peace to benefit from a good shock; it can be as simple as promoting ethical action in the community and being known for it if and when the shock comes.

In the aftermath of Young's successful negotiations, businesses started to ask themselves how they could instigate positive societal shifts – "good shocks" that realign the trajectories of their communities and themselves. Some companies even became active partners in community initiatives, aligning their CSR programs with the pursuit of societal change. Business leaders can engage in corporate diplomacy, building bridges with both established and emergent groups, ensuring communication lines remain open, allowing for essential discourse, understanding, and preparation as societal transformations take hold. This moral leadership sets an example not only by their goods and services but by their civic engagement and ethical practices.

In our hyper-connected age, a company's actions and stances are amplified and scrutinized like never before. Firms that contributed to humanitarian efforts, those that stood at the forefront of conservation, and those that embraced inclusivity found themselves on the right side of history – often setting the stage for "good shocks" and benefitting from their foresight. Gold Fields thrived by prioritizing ethical engagement and advocacy. The result was prosperity borne from a newfound legitimacy and trust. They became more than providers of products and services. They emerged as essential pillars elevating the societies in which they operate.

But being on the right side of history – or even making history – doesn't earn a company a perpetual pass. And building up trust doesn't mean it can't be squandered. What Young didn't count on was old guard executives at Gold Fields who wanted to use their newfound political power to build a total monopoly in South Africa like the bad old colonial days. They did it over Young's objections, and eventually the monopoly destroyed Gold Fields' reputation and almost ruined the company a decade later. This highlights a key problem when business engages directly in polycrisis: Society expects the firm to maintain its moral compass.

In the case of Zaki Khouri, herculean efforts in polycrisis can still fail. As of this writing, Hamas terrorists launched an attack from Gaza to target civilians with over 1,000 dead and hundreds taken hostage, which has triggered an unprecedented response – and resultant humanitarian crisis – in which Israel has killed over 30,000 Palestinians, the bulk of which are civilians. While warfare on civilians is not the majority view among Israelis or Palestinians, it is the view of those with the power to launch military attacks, and no company can stop combative leaders who are both desperate for total war.

The experiences of Gold Fields and NBC lead to a popular form of fatalism among business leaders about addressing the root causes of polycrisis: Why bother? In interviews, we found company leaders who understood exactly this problem. The main answer we found was that these leaders believed in the cause to their core and saw no other moral reaction.

The commitment to transparency, authenticity, and ethical practice plays a pivotal role in not only surviving but thriving amid societal upheaval. As businesses like Moreno's motorcycle shop demonstrated, unexpected alliances forged in the crucible of crisis can yield enduring benefits for all parties involved. Similarly, Young's work with Gold Fields showcases that embracing and facilitating positive societal changes – those "good shocks" – can serve as a catalyst for remarkable corporate success and legacy building.

The first crucial takeaway for leaders and leadership scholars is that it is possible for companies to address the root causes of polycrisis. Companies that stand steadfast by their well-founded values – those that prioritize actions that are consistent with their mission and principles – often sail through rough waters with a clear direction but can also help lessen the likelihood and impact of crises themselves.

Second, companies must be prepared to significantly address crises when they have social roots. Putting out a press release will only indicate where the company stands – it isn't the actual work of addressing the causes of crisis. Some companies are only able to make these kinds of statements. Others are on the "front lines" of the crisis itself and are uniquely positioned to support solving the problems that led to the crisis.

Third, while doing the work can be extremely rewarding, future managers can unwind even the greatest efforts. Gold Fields collapsed after Michael Young departed. Similarly, Moreno's efforts are still the efforts of only one shop and Khouri's efforts at NBC are only one company among many. Companies are part of intricate social systems that don't just require one actor to do one thing. It requires coordination, mutual support and joint effort. Negative consequences can cascade from one bad actor, even though positive consequences will usually need multiple actors working in concert. This is the fatalism that the most authentic and principled leaders are able to overcome.

Section Summary

Be it armed conflict or social conflict, there are three takeaway findings for leaders. The first is to **know your values**. Having a clear understanding of values enables leaders to make ethical decisions that align with core principles. When faced with a crisis but without a sure values footing, companies often prioritize short-term gains over long-term ethical considerations. However, companies that know their values can stay grounded and prioritize the well-being of their stakeholders to credibly uphold their ethical standards. By operating in alignment with their values, companies demonstrate their commitment to ethical behavior and build trust with stakeholders. This enhances a firm's reputation and strengthens its societal relationships. Furthermore, when leaders respond to crisis authentically and reflective of their organizational culture, trust and credibility are bolstered cyclically.

Second, **companies must act on their authentically held values, regardless of whether they are popular among all stakeholder groups.** The debates

over authentic leadership find expression in our work. Leaders who authentically strive to align their individual and work-related values, and who help other
stakeholders enact their true selves in work-related contexts, are more successful in weathering crises. Our sample is admittedly unique: They are leaders in
conflict contexts who spoke openly about their successes and failures. But our
work shows the promise of authentic leadership scholarship as applied to crisis
contexts.

Companies must act on their authentically held values, regardless of whether
they are popular. Authenticity in values-driven actions is crucial for maintaining
integrity and building trust. While it is important for companies to consider the
perspectives and interests of various stakeholders, blindly conforming to popular opinions can undermine the company's perception. Companies that act in
alignment with their authentic values are more likely to attract loyal customers,
dedicated employees, and investors. Companies can differentiate themselves in
the market and build a strong reputation based on consistent authenticity are
more likely to foster sustainable success and maintain stakeholder trust in the
long run.

Third, **companies must communicate their values AND their impartiality
in doing business with those they disagree with**. Authentically held beliefs
are unlikely to impact a company's ability to weather crisis unless they are
communicated. This is the time of greatest discomfort for many leaders:
Expressing values means opening up the company to other stakeholders –
particularly customers – expressing their disagreement, even revulsion. But
the communication of values must come with a clear message of impartiality.

In Chick-fil-A's case, support of Christian values did not mean they only
wanted Christian customers, only that they would operate their stores and spend
their money in accordance with their views. It tested emerging research arguing
that by communicating their values and impartiality, companies can soften the
impact of conflicts and boycotts, potentially even earning respect from stakeholders whose values are not aligned with their own.[49] Chick-fil-A's views
brought them into conflict with some segments of their customer base – and led
to boycotts – but their openness about the values and what they entailed also
softened the blow of those boycotts, even earning grudging respect from those
whose values were not in alignment.

Finally, **companies cannot rely on laws alone for their morality. In fact,
company's values may conflict with legal norms.** As we saw in Section 2,
relying on government guidance and legal norms alone can be disastrous. In this
Section, we saw how companies can benefit by moving beyond legal necessity.

---

[49] (Gold & Heikkurinen, 2018; Koskela & Camiciottoli, 2020).

Zahi Khouri and Hamdi Ulukaya discovered that going beyond laws can put a company on a collision course with a government in polarized environments. This tension can result in companies making strategic decisions that challenge the status quo, aligning more closely with their underlying principles than prescribed laws. Yet, stakeholders admire and support companies who demonstrate strong ethical standards.[50] Companies must navigate these pressures carefully, balancing their social responsibility with legal compliance, particularly amidst fluctuating political landscapes.

For a company to effectively navigate through polycrisis, they need to have the resolute composure to authentically stand by their core values, communicate these values transparently and impartially, and if required go beyond legal necessity in pursuit of corporate responsibility. Authenticity, communication, and the courage to challenge legal norms create trust and respect among stakeholders and position the company to better weather crisis, especially in highly polarized business environments.

---

[50] Sen & Bhattacharya (2001).

5 True Leadership in a World of Crisis

Business as Unusual[51]

Paul Polman squinted through the conference room windows at the Thames River eight stories below as managers awaited his directive. Dressed in a bespoke navy suit on this still-dim January morning, it was the Dutch transplant's first day as CEO of Unilever, the global consumer goods giant. He toyed silently with an audacious plan, one that no Fortune 500 firm had ever dared try before. His job, and the jobs of his ninety thousand employees, hung in the balance.

Crisis and panic embroiled the globe in this, the first full week of 2009. Competitors went bankrupt left and right. Talking heads on Bloomberg and the BBC guessed it was just weeks before Unilever joined them. Polman's first morning was a blur of managers delivering an endless drumbeat of bad news, convinced the world was collapsing. "Best practice" would have suggested that Polman's timing couldn't have been worse for a radical, fundamental change.

Polman's mission was clear: keep British households stocked with their Lipton tea, Dove soap, Hellmann's mayonnaise, and the rest of Unilever's hundreds of products. Polman had to save some of Britain's most beloved brands and the 140-year-old company behind them amid the worst global economic crisis in seventy years.

Polman had wanted to be a doctor then a priest, a calm life rooted in ethics. Somehow, he ended up in Ohio studying economics and working maintenance for Proctor and Gamble. He rose the ranks until Unilever hired him as CEO, his first leadership position. Now, Polman felt out of options: Shut down a division? Divest their Chinese operations? Furlough 20 percent of the workforce? Cut all R&D for the year? Picking wrong might only forestall the inevitable bankruptcy – or worse, accelerate it. The TV talking heads posited that he could do them all and it still might not be enough. Big institutional investors rang Polman's office nonstop, screaming to save their rapidly shrinking fiscal powder for a brighter day.

Polman needed to make a decision, fast.

---

[51] Sources for this section include: Polman, P., & Winston, A. (2021). *Net Positive: How Courageous Companies Thrive by Giving More than They Take.* Harvard: HBR Press; Financial Times, 2018, "High-flying Dutchman Polman divided opinion but leaves positive legacy." *Financial Times*, November 29; Saunders, A. (2011). "The MT Interview: Paul Polman of Unilever." *Management Today*; Daneshku, S. & Skapinker, M. (2016). "Can Unilever's Paul Polman change the way we do business?" *Financial Times*, September 29; Confino, J., (2011). "Paul Polman: The power is in the hands of the consumers." *Guardian*, November 21; Harvard Business Review. (2012). "Unilever's CEO on making responsible business work." Podcast, May 17; Harvard Business Review. (2012). "Captain Planet." June; Bell, G. (2013). "Doing well by doing good: An interview with Paul Polman, CEO of Unilever." (Two Parts). *Strategic Direction, 29*(4), 38–40.

His idea? To abolish quarterly reporting and guidance statements. Without them, investors couldn't assess the firm's true value in close to real-time. Polman saw that this reporting strangled firms. It forced them to endlessly prioritize short-term goals at the expense of more ethical actions that were more profitable for the company and better for society in the long term. And he wanted Unilever to do just that: Prioritize sustainability across the consumer goods giant so that they could become a net positive contributor to society and the environment.

He couldn't be fired on his first day. could he?

Polman put the order in. His managers sat silently, too shocked to argue. The next day, the market spoke loud and clear. Unilever's stock tanked 8 percent. Polman obliterated seven billion dollars in value after nine short hours on the job.

It got worse. For months, Polman ignored everyone who said he was fast-tracking the firm to ruin. He didn't shut down factories; he built more in the hardest-hit communities. He didn't burrow into a shell with the firm's cash hoard; he spent it on R&D to make more ethical products. Management experts thought it suicide. Unilever HQ teetered on the precipice of a riot.

Ninety-thousand employees, many of whom were having their homes foreclosed on, held their breath. Meanwhile, shareholders, battered by the poor performance of the rest of the market, screamed about earnings and quarterly reports. To Polman, the difference in these concerns showed what The Great Recession really was: not a crisis with economics or finance at its core, but what he called later a "crisis of ethics."

Unlike the suggestions of his managers, Polman built his plan on what he would later describe as "faith." His plan would test his beliefs – and try to make converts of his skeptical managers and shareholders. He began by eliminating quarterly earnings estimates to the public. This would reduce the desire of hedge funds and others "who would sell their grandmothers for a profit," as Polman would later say, from investing in the company. It would leave, for the most part, investors with a long-term view. Once the purge was complete, Polman offered a promise: Unilever would double its profits while halving its emissions in a little over a decade. The first part was outrageous enough; when coupled with the second, it seemed insane.

But by fall 2009, Unilever's sales and profits rocketed up 30 percent while competitors were either out of business or hopelessly hamstrung from penny pinching. As he rose through the corporate ranks at Unilever, Polman earned a reputation for not just paying lip service to the idea of business as a force for social good but also actually investing the money and hard work to make

positive change happen. Polman understood how business and society inter-
acted; worked with communities as partners; and then had the courage to act on
the findings for his company, even if they cost the firm in the short term.

Led by Polman, the Dutch/British conglomerate achieved what most pundits
thought impossible: integrating local community needs with long-term profitability and sustainability across hundreds of supply chains, seventy-five countries, and a dozen divisions. Polman did it by actively listening to fragile local
communities, seeing crisis as a constant feature of their business, shifting away
from quarterly profit/loss reporting to a longer-term perspective, and above all
else letting his subordinates dare to put social impact above profit. By the time
Polman retired in 2019, Unilever achieved both of Polman's insane 2008 goals.

Compare Polman's reaction to the financial crisis with that of General
Electric CEO Jeffrey Immelt. GE was co-founded by JP Morgan, who we saw
earlier expertly surveying political landscapes to succeed where Jay Cooke had
failed. But by the early 2000s, GE was the one making all the risky bets. The
results: A 42 percent decline in its stock price, slashing of dividends twice in
two years, the divestiture of most of the companies acquired in the lead-up to the
crisis, and the sale of $12 billion in shares in October 2008 to keep the company
afloat, which included a $3 billion, guaranteed dividend purchase by billionaire
Warren Buffet. GE became a shell of its former self, and never recovered.

Polman's Unilever experiences show what can happen when firms reassess
their leadership culture. Are they incorporating the crisis lessons we highlighted
in their executive hiring? Or are their values simply doublespeak like Altria's
claim they help their consumers by addicting them to cancer sticks, responsibly?
Most companies fall somewhere in the middle, but there's constant pressure to
lean towards the Altria variety. This is because the real work of values is simple in
theory but incredibly difficult in practice. It doesn't involve accounting proced-
ures or maximizing return on revenue or marketing a product better. It involves
searching into the soul of the organization, which is, after all, just a group of
people, to figure out the values that the group will live by in their work.

This Element's lessons are interlocking; together, they help explain why
companies succeed or fail during times of crisis and uncertainty. Our research
can help leaders understand what they need to do to steer through crises and help
scholars take leadership and crisis studies significantly forward. In its most
basic guise, company culture serves as the glue to bond the other two lessons.
Without the community engagement required from the social license and
insurance to operate and without an openness to their political roles, neither
company could create a crisis-proof culture. And without all three, companies
could never weather their respective storms. What we also see in both cases is
that, whether a company is starting from scratch with little direct experience

(NBC) or is highly experienced in the field with deep connections (Dilmah), the playbook is the same, and the culture must reflect community realities.

Technology Won't Save Us

That's not to say that past experiences can't rhyme with future debacles. Despite all our advances on corporate social responsibility and business engagement in and for society, Jay Cooke's experiences prove that the problems faced by Meta (previously Facebook), are anything but new, even as we stubbornly refuse to learn from our collective past mistakes.

Meta's gleaming 250-acre Menlo Park, California office complex is like a futuristic village, complete with wild foxes and an art museum. Sandwiched between the pinball machines and celebrity chef stations sits one of the world's most important societal change offices: Meta's Human Rights Division. This command center monitors billions of users around the globe with a singular mission: decipher if rebels, dictators, or other bad guys are using Meta to promote or commit atrocities. Meta's 10,000 employees are bombarded in the corridors and canteens with posters supporting the mission: "Err on the Side of Goodness" and "Be Better Together."

But here's the rub. Technology is only as useful as the people running it, and the man running Meta has a different motto that drives him: "Move Fast and Break Things." And in 2017, Meta broke something that a security patch couldn't fix.

In Myanmar, Meta was implicated in fomenting ethnic conflict under the full knowledge of CEO Mark Zuckerberg, even while Zuckerberg promised billions of dollars to build peace and "cure every disease." Meta ignored outside experts and its own human rights division that said that genocidaires were using the platform to recruit followers, dehumanize minority groups, and incite ethnic cleansing. After burying the findings for four years, Meta execs sheepishly fessed up and promised in a press release to do better, but only after their monopoly in the new market of 50 million people was secure. In response, the UN High Commissioner on Human Rights chastised them in a report on human rights abuses in Myanmar – the first time the Commissioner had ever implicated a tech company.

Meta is just one of hundreds of technology companies promising that their products will reshape lives for the better, but problems like Meta's in Myanmar aren't a bug – they're a feature. Social media models rely on the network effect: The idea that the product is only as valuable as the number of people who use it. Meta is like a telephone in that anyone can use it. The difference between the telephone and a social media company like Meta is how the company makes money. Telephone users are charged by the call. It doesn't matter if the call is to wish a loved one happy birthday or to order the killing of a rebel leader – the price is the same.

But social media companies make their money when people click on ads; they are purpose-built to supercharge incendiary content. The more extreme the ads, the more likely they are to be clicked. Meta management knows that every evil campaign they host guts their credibility, but they're incapable of giving up the dopamine rush brought by each documented increase in engagement. Worse, the $250 billion company with ten million users in conflict-ridden Myanmar didn't have a single Burmese employee. Everything was run out of Menlo Park or a three-expat strong Yangon field office. Their social exposure was equivalent to entering an uninsured Lamborghini into a demolition derby. Catastrophe wasn't just possible – it was inevitable.

Caught between regulators in democratic countries who see them as a threat to democratic speech and dictatorial regimes who use their products to control their population, companies that refuse to regulate themselves risk implosion. While few might shed a tear over Meta, hundreds of thousands of businesses rely exclusively on social media for customers, spending years to build those connections. If Meta's plug is pulled, thousands of companies will go out of business.

This last point represents one of our most important takeaways: Our poly-crisis environment impacts *everyone*, and reconceptualizing risk means thinking about it in not only a new way but also most often in a way that's diametrically opposed to how leading firms of the moment do. Meta's move-fast-and-break-things strategy has real world consequences. When the things broken are human lives, a company trying to pay for its social insurance would take responsibility. But not Meta. They continue to do legal and mental gymnastics to sidestep blame for the lives their platform has destroyed. And consumers, communities, plaintiffs, and governments will all eventually come knocking for blood money – just as they've done for the cigarette and chemical firms of previous generations that spent more time fighting allegations of social harm than trying to fix their operations.

Is it too late for Meta? We ourselves have argued yes.[52] But we've also learned that even the most socially broken businesses can be repaired by leadership that prioritizes social and environmental impact. Unilever before Paul Polman was not the model of success that it became under his leadership. If anything, as one of the largest consumer goods companies in the world, it was often the case of environmental problems in some of the world's poorest communities. Polman's vision to make Unilever sustainable was ambitious and achievable. Under his leadership it worked. The ability to change is in the

---

[52] See for example, Katsos & Miklian (2021).

hands of leadership. As proof, many of Unilever's sustainability impacts dwindled after Polman's retirement from the C-suite.

Concluding Thoughts

Our research and its practical applications can help leaders better navigate polycrisis settings. Our findings aren't a checklist or a to-do style prescription for success through crisis. They're reminders that doing the right thing for society is the same as both the prepared thing *and* the profitable thing.

Just as we have stood on the shoulders of giants in our scholarly work, it is essential that today's research encourages the next generation of scholars to more deeply tackle business and crisis concerns. Returning to the statistic that less than 3 percent of business and management scholarly articles are concerned with analyses of "grand challenges" or "wicked problems," we see three specific areas where this research can add forward value.

First, we need more research on the relationships between business ethics and leadership roles under polycrisis. We have a great deal of literature on leadership and ethics dynamics during a singular crisis, but our research suggests that polycrisis environments carry unique characteristics that can challenge or expand the conditional value of our existing understandings of crisis leadership research. For leaders and managers in larger firms especially, betting the right tools to be able to see overlapping crisis effects – and not compartmentalizing them amongst divisions that don't speak much to each other – will be key to developing truly impactful crisis management strategies.

Second, connecting peace and conflict studies with leader emotions and psychology can expand polycrisis understandings. Humans have specialized psychological mechanisms for solving coordination problems through leadership and followership,[53] so different leadership styles are needed depending on the type of crisis, necessitating varied competencies and a crisis-prone culture within organizations. Cross-disciplinary work can explore these issues empirically by connecting subdisciplines between political science, management, leader psychology, and conflict/fragility studies. To wit, Jason comes from a political science and development studies background. John's background is in business-management and law. It took all four of these disciplines to simply seek out good questions in our qualitative research, let alone understand causes and consequences.

---

[53] This perspective provides insights into the barriers to leadership effectiveness in organizations with conceptual frameworks that align leadership, culture, and crisis management with each stage of crisis management and types of crisis (Bhaduri, 2019b). Also see Rettberg (2016) for political science, Little et al. (2016) and Toegel et al. (2013) in mgmt; also see van Vugt & Ronay (2013) and Bhaduri (2019b).

Third, we need to zoom out to the big sociopolitical picture, and that means engaging with those who live these experiences. But that doesn't mean that firms need to be social workers or knowledge hubs rivaling that of top university programs. Leaders have myriad competing demands on their time and resources. Our aim is not to give them one more thing to do or chide them for one best practice that they don't have the time or resources to undertake.

Instead, we unite aspects of a company that may seem disparate or haphazard but need to be united to make actionable, sustainable, and profitable decisions in times of crisis. The default stance of many companies is the default stance for most of us as human beings: panic. Many companies even adopt special crisis terminology such as "all hands on deck" and "batten down the hatches," which always seem to be nautically-themed. And perhaps that's appropriate.

On the sea as in business, a rising tide lifts all boats so long as it's paired with calm weather. When things are going well, most firms do well. The inverse is not always true. When the weather is rough, many firms sink. Our current situation is akin to hurricane season. We don't know exactly when the next one will come – but it is coming. We also don't know the severity or frequency – we might have plenty of time between them to recover or none at all.

We saw companies thrive in terrible operating environments. From Merrill Fernando's Dilmah Tea in civil war Sri Lanka to Zaki Khouri's NBC in Gaza after the Oslo Peace Accords, the stories of success in the world's hardest places are lessons for every business trying to weather crisis. And as we saw with Jay Cooke, these seasons of crisis last an indeterminate length and can seemingly spring up out of nowhere. For Dilmah Tea in Sri Lanka, it lasted twenty-five years. For Tata, it was a decade. For Juan Valdez, it's been half a century.

What makes this time even more challenging is that it requires global action. Returning to the mega-challenges we discussed in the introduction, fixing inequality in America won't solve global inequality between those in rich countries and those not. Globalization heightens that challenge by exacerbating interconnections between one place and every other place. Climate change adds extreme and unpredictable environmental and sociopolitical stresses that are hard to predict and, like the old "butterfly flaps its wings" cliché, can reverberate in ways and places far afield from where disasters strike.

Companies need to look to their communities to weather new storms and will need to match the underlying causes of crisis – inequality, climate change, and globalization. But leaders should not attempt to create a one-size-fits-all social license and insurance plan. These will not necessarily be scalable solutions. Instead, companies will have to start doing the terrifying work of listening to people. We saw in Section Three that these activities are usually the first ones sidelined to standardize community engagement through principles sponsored by international institutions. But what a local community needs are the local community, not some suited figure in a golden ballroom thousands of miles away.

After all, crisis is not just the number of dead or a state of politics; it is a state of upheaval and chaos. And it's easy to see how the world is teetering towards a general state of upheaval and chaos. Many in the developed and developing world are unused to constant crisis in their operating environment. While we hope for a return to a time of more stability, globalization, climate change, and income inequality are going to make for a rough few decades. Our research suggests that the best way for a firm to thrive is to be ready for constant crisis in the everything.

Appendix
Methodology and Limitations

Our secondary data collection analyzed two hundred official documents from the United Nations, national governments, multilateral agencies, think tanks, and research centers on the role of business in crisis. We processed over 250 academic articles, practitioner pieces, and books on business in conflict and crisis and compiled them into a meta-analysis of scholarly best practices. Sources of particular relevance and merit are presented throughout.

Specific empirical methodologies of our extracted works include process tracing (Miklian, 2014), ethnographic study of vulnerable populations (Miklian, 2009, 2012; Ganson, 2019), open-ended interviews of managers (Katsos, 2019; Katsos & AlKafaji, 2019) grounded research on sociopolitical factors (Miklian & Carney, 2013; Miklian & Hoelscher, 2016; Miklian & Medina Bickel, 2020), C-Suite interviews (Katsos & Fort, 2016; Katsos et al., 2021), survey instruments (Miklian & Hoelscher, 2018; Barkemeyer & Miklian, 2019); qualitative theory building (Hoelscher et al., 2012, 2017); and conceptual papers (Miklian, 2017; Miklian, Alluri, et al., 2019; Miklian, Journal, et al., 2019; Miklian & Schouten, 2019; Ganson et al., 2022). Correlations of findings across methodological disciplines and subfields provide evidence for their validity.[1]

We see three important limitations: selection bias, causal analysis claims, and the limitations of advanced methods in conflict settings. First, while this work focuses upon case studies of firms succeeding or failing, picking a few winners doesn't constitute empirical proof. Our selection process was of best case fit but also reflects lessons of firms we studied that *didn't* succeed. This process intended to illustrate the *why* of those processes, not of a singular strategy. Still, leaning too heavily on success stories may give the impression that their success wasn't also at least partially due to random good fortune. Therefore, we stressed the *how* of success, to help understand how leaders may have been able to make this luck, even if it is impossible to prove (or disprove) that these specific actions made the difference.

This approach aligns with qualitative research strategies in the social sciences that stress the difficulty in testing causal chains in sociopolitical study. Process tracing methodology has a rich tradition in political science (e.g., Gerring

---

[1] For those seeking additional detail on methodology, we encourage readings of these specific case articles, many of which contain sophisticated methodological discussions that we need not repeat here. All articles are either Open Access or available upon request to the authors.

2012), as we employed in case studies. For other studies, like survey work, our findings opened discussions amongst actors in polycrisis settings of how certain actions by leaders were correlated with more positive firm and community outcomes, but we stop short of making specific causal claims (x action caused y result). We see this as an opportunity for future research, as empirical testing can test many of the correlations that we have observed to help expand our understanding of leadership in crisis.

Moreover, when researching complex social processes, difficult questions regarding form and format of how we can most robustly develop theory and defend our results invariably arise. And any methodology – qualitative or quantitative – is more difficult in crisis settings, where sociopolitical ties are strained and more opaque than in "standard" settings. Therefore, we connect qualitative and quantitative evidence with case studies on leaders whose stories are emblematic of the lessons that can be drawn from the evidence. However, given the variety of cases and methods, we aimed to use this evidence base only to show how old strategies fail and give some insight into strategies that explore how they can succeed.

References

Ansell, C., & Boin, A. (2019). Taming deep uncertainty: The potential of pragmatist principles for understanding and improving strategic crisis management. *Administration and Society, 51*(7), 1079–1112. https://doi.org/10.1177/0095399717747655

Babalola, M. T., Stouten, J., Euwema, M. C., & Ovadje, F. (2018). The relation between ethical leadership and workplace conflicts: The mediating role of employee resolution efficacy. *Journal of Management, 44*(5), 2037–2063. https://doi.org/10.1177/0149206316638163

Baden, D. (2016). A reconstruction of Carroll's pyramid of corporate social responsibility for the 21st century. *International Journal of Corporate Social Responsibility, 1*(1). https://doi.org/10.1186/S40991-016-0008-2

Barkemeyer, R., & Miklian, J. (2019). Responsible business in fragile contexts: Comparing perceptions from domestic and foreign firms in Myanmar. *Sustainability, 11*(3), 598. https://doi.org/10.3390/su11030598

Baskerville, R., Spagnoletti, P., & Kim, J. (2014). Incident-centered information security: Managing a strategic balance between prevention and response. *Information & Management, 51*(1), 138–151. https://doi.org/10.1016/J.IM.2013.11.004

Bass, B., & Avolio, B. (1993). Transformational leadership and organizational culture on Jstor. *Public Administration Quarterly, 17*(1), 112–121. www.jstor.org/stable/40862298

Bauman, D. C. (2011). Evaluating ethical approaches to crisis leadership: Insights from unintentional harm research. *Journal of Business Ethics, 98*(2), 281–295. https://doi.org/10.1007/S10551-010-0549-3/METRICS

Belitski, M., Guenther, C., Kritikos, A. S., & Thurik, R. (2021). Economic effects of the COVID-19 pandemic on entrepreneurship and small businesses. *SSRN Electronic Journal.* https://doi.org/10.2139/SSRN.3899010

Bhaduri, R. M. (2019a). Leveraging culture and leadership in crisis management. *European Journal of Training and Development, 43*(5–6), 554–569. https://doi.org/10.1108/EJTD-10-2018-0109

Bhaduri, R. M. (2019b). Leveraging culture and leadership in crisis management. *European Journal of Training and Development, 43*(5–6), 554–569. https://doi.org/10.1108/EJTD-10-2018-0109/FULL/XML

Bowen, F., Newenham-Kahindi, A., & Herremans, I. (2010). When suits meet roots: The antecedents and consequences of community engagement strategy. *Journal of Business Ethics*, *95*(2), 297–318. https://doi.org/10.1007/S10551-009-0360-1

Bratianu, C. (2020). Toward understanding the complexity of the COVID-19 crisis: A grounded theory approach. *Management and Marketing*, *15*(s1), 410–423. https://doi.org/10.2478/MMCKS-2020-0024

Brown, M. E., & Treviño, L. K. (2006). Ethical leadership: A review and future directions. *Leadership Quarterly*, *17*(6), 595–616. https://doi.org/10.1016/j.leaqua.2006.10.004

Cakir, M., Wardman, J., Analysis, A. T.-R., & 2022, undefined. (2022). Ethical leadership supports safety voice by increasing risk perception and reducing ethical ambiguity: Evidence from the COVID-19 pandemic. *Wiley Online Library*. https://doi.org/10.1111/risa.14053

Caringal-Go, J. F., Teng-Calleja, M., Franco, E. P., Manaois, J. O., & Zantua, R. M. S. (2021). Crisis leadership from the perspective of employees during the COVID-19 pandemic. *Leadership and Organization Development Journal*, *42*(4), 630–643. https://doi.org/10.1108/LODJ-07-2020-0284/FULL/XML

Carroll, A. B., & Shabana, K. M. (2010). The business case for corporate social responsibility: A review of concepts, research and practice. *International Journal of Management Reviews*, *12*(1), 85–105. https://doi.org/10.1111/J.1468-2370.2009.00275.X

Chakraborty, A., & Jha, A. (2019). Corporate social responsibility in marketing: A review of the state-of-the-art literature. *Journal of Social Marketing*, *9*(4), 418–446. https://doi.org/10.1108/JSOCM-01-2019-0005/FULL/PDF

Cho, M., Furey, L. D., & Mohr, T. (2016). Communicating corporate social responsibility on social media. Http://Dx.Doi.Org/10.1177/2329490616663708, 80(1), 52–69. https://doi.org/10.1177/2329490616663708

Choflet, A., Packard, T., Hospital, K. S.-J. of, & 2021, undefined. (2021). Rethinking organizational change in the COVID-19 era. *Researchgate. NetA Choflet, T Packard, K StashowerJournal of Hospital Management and Health Policy, 2021•researchgate.Net*, *5*(June). https://doi.org/10.21037/jhmhp-21-11

Christensen, S., Society, J. K.-B., & 2003, undefined. (2008). Ethical decision making in times of organizational crisis: A framework for analysis. *Journals.Sagepub.ComSL Christensen, J KohlsBusiness & Society, 2003•journals.Sagepub.Com*, *42*(3), 328–358. https://doi.org/10.1177/0007650303255855

Ciulla, J., Price, T., Murphy, S., (Eds.) (2008). *The Quest for Moral Leaders*. London: Edward Elgar.

Clarke, S. (1990). The crisis of fordism or the crisis of social-democracy? *Telos*, *1990*(83), 71–98. https://doi.org/10.3817/0390083071

Coca-Cola touts its Palestinian employment creds amid boycott calls. (n.d.). Retrieved July 18, 2023, from https://malaysia.news.yahoo.com/coca-cola-touts-palestinian-employment-045900579.html

Coldwell, D. A. L. (2017). Ethical leadership in crisis management: The role of university education. *Contemporary Leadership Challenges*. https://doi.org/10.5772/65497

Cole, J. C., & Roberts, J. T. (2011). Lost opportunities? A comparative assessment of social development elements of six hydroelectricity CDM projects in Brazil and Peru. Https://Doi.Org/10.1080/17565529.2011.623831, *3*(4), 361–379. https://doi.org/10.1080/17565529.2011.623831

Collier, J., & Esteban, R. (2007). Corporate social responsibility and employee commitment. *Business Ethics: A European Review*, *16*(1), 19–33. https://doi.org/10.1111/J.1467-8608.2006.00466.X

compass, R. C.-G., & 2017, undefined. (2017). Towards a critical geography of disaster recovery politics: Perspectives on crisis and hope. *Wiley Online Library*, *11*(1). https://doi.org/10.1111/gec3.12302

Cordero, R. (2016). Crisis and critique: On the fragile foundations of social life. *Crisis and Critique: On the Fragile Foundations of Social Life*, 1–186. https://doi.org/10.4324/9781315753904/CRISIS-CRITIQUE-RODRIGO-CORDERO

Corral de Zubielqui, G., & Harris, H. (2023). Why the COVID-19 crisis is an ethical issue for business: Evidence from the Australian JobKeeper initiative. *Journal of Business Ethics*. https://doi.org/10.1007/S10551-023-05392-2

de Andrade Melim-McLeod, C. (2018). Managing water (in)security in Brazil: Lessons from a megacity. *Climate Change Management*, 413–427. https://doi.org/10.1007/978-3-319-56946-8_25

Dean, D. H. (2004). Consumer reaction to negative publicity: Effects of corporate reputation, response, and responsibility for a crisis event. *Journal of Business Communication*, *41*(2), 192–211. https://doi.org/10.1177/0021943603261748

Demuijnck, G., & Fasterling, B. (2016). The social license to operate. *Journal of Business Ethics*, *136*(4), 675–685. https://doi.org/10.1007/S10551-015-2976-7

DL Deephouse, P. J. (2013). Do family firms have better reputations than non-family firms? An integration of socioemotional wealth and social identity theories. *Journal of Management Studies*, *50*(3), 337–360.

Dubey, R. (2022). Unleashing the potential of digital technologies in emergency supply chain: The moderating effect of crisis leadership. *Industrial*

Management and Data Systems, *123*(1), 112–132. https://doi.org/10.1108/IMDS-05-2022-0307/FULL/XML

Eggers, F. (2020). Masters of disasters? Challenges and opportunities for SMEs in times of crisis. *Journal of Business Research*, *116*, 199–208. https://doi.org/10.1016/J.JBUSRES.2020.05.025

Eweje, G., & Brunton, M. (2010). Ethical perceptions of business students in a New Zealand university: Do gender, age and work experience matter? *Business Ethics*, *19*(1), 95–111. https://doi.org/10.1111/J.1467-8608.2009.01581.X

Farrington, A. (2002). Trading places: The East India Company and Asia. *History Today*, *52*(5), 40–41. https://doi.org/10.1386/IJFS.5.2.131

Faugère, C., & Gergaud, O. (2017). Business ethics searches: A socioeconomic and demographic analysis of U.S. Google Trends in the context of the 2008 financial crisis. *Business Ethics*, *26*(3), 271–287. https://doi.org/10.1111/BEER.12138

Ganson, B. (2019). Business and peace. In *Business, Peacebuilding and Sustainable Development* (pp. 3–26). https://doi.org/10.4324/9780429057229-1

Ganson, B., He, T. L., & Henisz, W. J. (2022). Business and peace: The impact of firm–stakeholder relational strategies on conflict risk. Https://Doi.Org/10.5465/Amr.2019.0411, *47*(2), 259–281. https://doi.org/10.5465/AMR.2019.0411

Ganson, B., & Wennmann, A. (2012). *Operationalising Conflict Prevention as Strong, Resilient Systems: Approaches, Evidence, Action Points*. https://repository.graduateinstitute.ch/record/288057/files/GPP_P_03_2012.pdf

Gehman, J., Lefsrud, L., Public, S. F.-C., & 2017, undefined. (2017). Social license to operate: Legitimacy by another name? *Wiley Online Library*, *60*(2), 293–317. https://doi.org/10.1111/capa.12218

Gigol, T., Kreczmanska-Gigol, K., & Pajewska-Kwasny, R. (2021). Socially responsible leadership's impact on stakeholder management, staff job satisfaction and work engagement. *European Research Studies Journal*, *XXIV* (Special Issue 4), 775–805. https://doi.org/10.35808/ERSJ/2805

Gold, S., & Heikkurinen, P. (2018). Transparency fallacy: Unintended consequences of stakeholder claims on responsibility in supply chains. *Accounting, Auditing and Accountability Journal*, *31*(1), 318–337. https://doi.org/10.1108/AAAJ-06-2015-2088/FULL/XML

Gruss, R., Kim, E., & Abrahams, A. (2020). Engaging restaurant customers on Facebook: The power of belongingness appeals on social media. *Journal of Hospitality and Tourism Research*, *44*(2), 201–228. https://doi.org/10.1177/1096348019892071

Guibert, L., & Roloff, J. (2017). Stakeholder dialogue: Strategic tool or wasted words? *Journal of Business Strategy*, *38*(5), 3–11. https://doi.org/10.1108/JBS-07-2016-0071/FULL/XML

Hackett, R. D., & Wang, G. (2012). Virtues and leadership: An integrating conceptual framework founded in Aristotelian and Confucian perspectives on virtues. *Management Decision*, *50*(5), 868–899.

Henig, D., & Knight, D. (2023). Polycrisis: Anthropological prompts for an emerging worldview. *Anthropology Today*, *39*(2), 3–6. https://doi.org/10.1111/1467-8322.12793

Herbane, B. (2010). Small business research: Time for a crisis-based view. Http://Dx.Doi.Org/10.1177/0266242609350804, *28*(1), 43–64. https://doi.org/10.1177/02662426093508041

Hoelscher, K., Miklian, J., Håvard, Nygård, M., & Nygård, H. M. (2017). Conflict, peacekeeping, and humanitarian security: Understanding violent attacks against aid workers. *Taylor & Francis*, *24*(4), 538–565. https://doi.org/10.1080/13533312.2017.1321958

Hoelscher, K., Miklian, J., & Vadlamannati, K. C. (2012). Hearts and mines: A district-level analysis of the Maoist conflict in India. *International Area Studies Review*, *15*(2), 141–160. https://doi.org/10.1177/2233865912447022

Hoyer, D., Bennett, J., Reddish, J., Holder, S., & Howard, R. (2023). *Navigating Polycrisis: Long-Run Socio-Cultural Factors Shape Response to Changing Climate.* https://osf.io/h6kma/download

Jiang, H., & Luo, Y. (2018). Crafting employee trust: From authenticity, transparency to engagement. *Journal of Communication Management*, *22* (2), 138–160. https://doi.org/10.1108/JCOM-07-2016-0055/FULL/XML

Joniaková, Z., Jankelová, N., Blštáková, J., & Némethová, I. (2021). Cognitive diversity as the quality of leadership in crisis: Team performance in health service during the COVID-19 pandemic. *Healthcare*, *9*(3), 313. https://doi.org/10.3390/HEALTHCARE9030313

Joseph, J., Katsos, J. E., & Daher, M. (2020). Local business, local peace? Intergroup and economic dynamics. *Journal of Business Ethics*, *173*(4), 835–854. https://doi.org/10.1007/s10551-020-04515-3

journal, B. H.-I. small business, & 2010, undefined. (2010). Small business research: Time for a crisis-based view. *Journals.Sagepub.ComB HerbaneInternational Small Business Journal, 2010•journals.Sagepub.Com*, *28*(1), 43–64. https://doi.org/10.1177/0266242609350804

Kassem, R., Ajmal, M., Gunasekaran, A., & Helo, P. (2019). Assessing the impact of organizational culture on achieving business excellence with a moderating role of ICT: An SEM approach. *Benchmarking*, *26*(1), 117–146. https://doi.org/10.1108/BIJ-03-2018-0068/FULL/PDF

Katsos, J. E. (2019). Business and terrorism: The ISIS case. In J. E. Katsos, J. Miklian, & R. M. Alluri (Eds.), *Business, Peacebuilding and Sustainable Development*. Routledge.

Katsos, J. E., & AlKafaji, Y. (2019). Business in war zones: How companies promote peace in Iraq. *Journal of Business Ethics, 155*(1), 41–56. https://doi .org/10.1007/s10551-017-3513-7

Katsos, J. E., & Forrer, J. (2014). Business practices and peace in post-conflict zones: Lessons from Cyprus. *Business Ethics, 23*(2), 154–168. https://doi .org/10.1111/beer.12044

Katsos, J. E., & Fort, T. L. (2016). Leadership in the promotion of peace: Interviews with the 2015 business for peace honorees. *Business Horizons, 59*(5), 463–470. https://doi.org/10.1016/J.BUSHOR.2016.03.010

Katsos, J., & Miklian, J. (2021). *A New Crisis Playbook for an Uncertain World. We're Entering a Period of Unprecedented Instability. Is Your Business Prepared?* https://pure.qub.ac.uk/en/publications/a-new-crisis-playbook-for-an-uncertain-world-were-entering-a-peri

Katsos, J., Miklian, J., & McClelland, P. (2021). *Building a Culture that Can Withstand a Crisis. How a Company that Works in Conflict Zones Prepares for the Unknown.* https://pure.qub.ac.uk/en/publications/building-a-culture-that-can-withstand-a-crisis-how-a-company-that

Knight, D., Today, D. H.-A., & 2023, undefined. (2023). Polycrisis: Anthropological prompts for an emerging worldview. *Research-Repository. St-Andrews.Ac . . . , 39*(2), 3–6. https://doi.org/10.1111/1467-8322.12793

Koselleck, C. R. (1988). Critique and crisis: Enlightenment and the pathogenesis of modern society. In *History of European Ideas* (Issue 6). MIT Press. https://doi.org/10.1016/0191-6599(88)90132-5

Koskela, M., & Camiciottoli, B. C. (2020). Different paths from transparency to trust? A comparative analysis of Finnish and Italian listed companies' investor relations communication practices. *Studies in Communication Sciences, 20*(1), 59–76. https://doi.org/10.24434/j.scoms.2020.01.006

Landrum, N. E., & Ohsowski, B. (2018). Identifying worldviews on corporate sustainability: A content analysis of corporate sustainability reports. *Business Strategy and the Environment, 27*(1), 128–151. https://doi.org/10.1002/ BSE.1989

Laschewski, L., Phillipson, J., & Gorton, M. (2002). The facilitation and formalisation of small business networks: Evidence from the north east of England. Http:// Dx.Doi.Org/10.1068/C0066a, *20*(3), 375–391. https://doi.org/10.1068/C0066A

Lumpkin, G. T., & Dess, G. G. (1996). Clarifying the entrepreneurial orientation construct and linking it to performance. *The Academy of Management Review, 21*(1), 135. https://doi.org/10.2307/258632

Magrizos, S., Apospori, E., Carrigan, M., & Jones, R. (2021). Is CSR the panacea for SMEs? A study of socially responsible SMEs during economic crisis. *European Management Journal, 39*(2), 291–303. https://doi.org/ 10.1016/J.EMJ.2020.06.002

Mahdani, I., Saputra, J., Adam, M., & Yunus, M. (n.d.). *Organizational Culture, Employee Motivation, Workload and Employee Performance: A Mediating Role of Communication.* https://doi.org/10.37394/23207.2022.19.6

Manuel, T., & Herron, T. L. (2020). An ethical perspective of business CSR and the COVID-19 pandemic. *Society and Business Review, 15*(3), 235–253. https://doi.org/10.1108/SBR-06-2020-0086

Marques, T., Reis, N., & Gomes, J. F. S. (2018). Responsible leadership research: A bibliometric review. *BAR – Brazilian Administration Review, 15*(1), e170112. https://doi.org/10.1590/1807-7692BAR2018170112

Mayer, D. M., Kuenzi, M., & Greenbaum, R. L. (2010). Examining the link between ethical leadership and employee misconduct: The mediating role of ethical climate. *Journal of Business Ethics, 95*(Suppl. 1), 7–16. https://doi .org/10.1007/S10551-011-0794-0/METRICS

Miklian, J. (2009). The purification hunt: The Salwa Judum counterinsurgency in Chhattisgarh, India. *Dialectical Anthropology, 33*(3–4), 441–459. https:// doi.org/10.1007/S10624-009-9138-1

Miklian, J. (2012). The political ecology of war in Maoist India. *Politics, Religion & Ideology,* 13(4), 561–576. https://doi.org/10.1080/ 21567689.2012.732017

Miklian, J. (2014). The past, present and future of the "Liberal Peace." *Strategic Analysis, 38*(4), 493–507. www.researchgate.net/profile/Jason_Miklian/pub lication/264350109_The_Past_Present_and_Future_of_the_% 27Liberal_Peace%27/links/5716dd9408aec49c999cc3d6/The-Past-Present- and-Future-of-the-Liberal-Peace.pdf

Miklian, J. (2017). Mapping business-peace interactions: Opportunities and recommendations. *Business, Peace and Sustainable Development, 2017* (10), 3–27. https://doi.org/10.9774/TandF.8757.2017.de.00002

Miklian, J., Alluri, R. M., & Katsos, J. E. (2019). *Business, Peacebuilding and Sustainable Development.* Routledge. https://books.google.ae/books? id=6KeaDwAAQBAJ

Miklian, J., & Carney, S. (2013). Corruption, justice and violence in democratic India. *SAIS Review of International Affairs, 33*(1), 37–49. www.academia .edu/download/34707007/Miklian_Carney_corruption_India.pdf

Miklian, J., & Hoelscher, K. (2016). The evolution of the smart cities agenda in India. *Journals.Sagepub.Com, 19*(1), 28–44. https://doi.org/10.1177/ 2233865916632089

Miklian, J., & Hoelscher, K. (2018). A new research approach for Peace Innovation. *Innovation and Development, 8*(2), 189–207. https://rsa.tandfon line.com/doi/full/10.1080/2157930X.2017.1349580

Miklian, J., Journal, K. H.-I. S. B., & 2022, undefined. (2019). SMEs and exogenous shocks: A conceptual literature review and forward research agenda. *Journals.Sagepub.ComJ Miklian, K HoelscherInternational Small Business Journal, 2022•journals.Sagepub.Com, 2022*(2), 178–204. https:// doi.org/10.1177/02662426211050796

Miklian, J., & Medina Bickel, J. P. (2020). Theorizing business and local peacebuilding through the "footprints of peace" coffee project in rural Colombia. *Business and Society, 59*(4), 676–715. https://doi.org/10.1177/ 0007650317749441

Miklian, J., & Schouten, P. (2019). Broadening "business," widening "peace": A new research agenda on business and peace-building. *Conflict, Security and Development, 19*(1), 1–13. https://doi.org/10.1080/14678802 .2019.1561612

Morgan, G., Barnwell, G., Johnstone, L., & Shukla, K. (2022). The power threat meaning framework and the climate and ecological crises. *Psychology in Society.* https://leicester.figshare.com/articles/journal_contribution/ The_Power_Threat_Meaning_Framework_and_the_climate_and_ecologica l_crises/21711860

Mullings, B., & Otuomagie, T. (2023). Resilience in the context of multiple crises. In *Encyclopedia of the Social and Solidarity Economy.* https://books.google.com/ books?hl=en&lr=&id=gt65EAAAQBAJ&oi=fnd&pg=PA409&dq=Mullings +and+Otuomagie+2023&ots=7blfz1Maqv&sig=6_Um-bCAsZw8W3gC5_ IvEOvjmg8

Murshed, S. M. (2022). Consequences of the Covid-19 pandemic for economic inequality. In *COVID-19 and International Development* (pp. 59–70). Springer International. https://doi.org/10.1007/978-3-030-82339-9_5/ FIGURES/1

Newstead, T., & Riggio, R. (2023). *Leadership and Virtues: Understanding and Practicing Good Leadership.* New York: Taylor and Francis.

Nikiforou, A. (Iro), Lioukas, S., Chatzopoulou, E. C., & Voudouris, I. (2023). When there is a crisis, there is an opportunity? SMEs' capabilities for durability and opportunity confidence. *International Journal of Entrepreneurial Behaviour and Research, 29*(5), 1053–1074. https://doi .org/10.1108/IJEBR-11-2021-0939

Nikolova, N., & Andersen, L. (2017). Creating shared value through service-learning in management education. Http://Dx.Doi.Org/10.1177/

1052562917715883, *41*(5), 750–780. https://doi.org/10.1177/1052562917 715883

Obrenovic, B., Du, J., Godinic, D., et al. (2020). Sustaining enterprise operations and productivity during the COVID-19 pandemic: "Enterprise effectiveness and sustainability model." *Sustainability, 12*(15), 5981. https://doi.org/10.3390/SU12155981

Oh, J., Cho, D., & Lim, D. H. (2018). Authentic leadership and work engagement: The mediating effect of practicing core values. *Leadership and Organization Development Journal, 39*(2), 276–290. https://doi.org/10.1108/LODJ-02-2016-0030/FULL/XML

Okpara, J. O. (2014). The effects of national culture on managers' attitudes toward business ethics: Implications for organizational change. *Journal of Accounting and Organizational Change, 10*(2), 174–189. https://doi.org/10.1108/JAOC-07-2012-0046

Orr, Z., Jackson, L., Alpert, E. A., & Fleming, M. D. (2022). Neutrality, conflict, and structural determinants of health in a Jerusalem emergency department. *International Journal for Equity in Health, 21*(1), 1–12. https://doi.org/10.1186/S12939-022-01681-W/METRICS

Panwar, R., Paul, K., Nybakk, E., Hansen, E., & Thompson, D. (2014). The legitimacy of CSR actions of publicly traded companies versus family-owned companies. *Journal of Business Ethics, 125*(3), 481–496. https://doi.org/10.1007/S10551-013-1933-6/TABLES/5

Pappas, N. (2018). Hotel decision-making during multiple crises: A chaordic perspective. *Tourism Management, 68*, 450–464. https://doi.org/10.1016/J.TOURMAN.2018.04.009

Parmar, B. L., Freeman, R. E., Harrison, J. S., et al. (2010). Stakeholder theory: The state of the art. *Academy of Management Annals, 4*(1), 403–445. https://doi.org/10.5465/19416520.2010.495581

Pérez, A., & Bosque, I. R. del. (2014). Customer CSR expectations in the banking industry. *International Journal of Bank Marketing, 32*(3), 223–244. https://doi.org/10.1108/IJBM-09-2013-0095

Perrow, C. (2011). Normal accidents: Living with high risk technologies. In *Normal Accidents: Living with High Risk Technologies*, 1–451. https://doi.org/10.2307/3105374

Pettigrew, W., & Gopalan, M. (2016). *The East India Company, 1600–1857: Essays on Anglo-Indian Connection.* https://books.google.com/books?hl=en&lr=&id=6ZKuDAAAQBAJ&oi=fnd&pg=PP1&dq=Pettigrew,+W.+and+Gopalan,+M,+2016.+The+East+India+Company,+1600–1857:+Essays+on+Anglo-Indian+Connection&ots=_PU8mwE4Gj&sig=-AhYpYBYtUyzqDaR1acWPQ_ssgw

Piereder, J., Janzwood, S., & Homer-Dixon, T. (2022). Ideology and climate change. In *The Routledge Handbook of Ideology and International Relations*, 267–295. https://doi.org/10.4324/9781003026754-19

Pless, N. M., & Maak, T. (2012). Responsible leadership: Pathways to the future. *Responsible Leadership*, *98*(1), 3–13. https://doi.org/10.1007/S10551-011-1114-4/METRICS

Price, G., & van der Walt, A. J. (2013). Changes in attitudes towards business ethics held by former South African business management students. *Journal of Business Ethics*, *113*(3), 429–440. https://doi.org/10.1007/S10551-012-1314-6

Qi, L., & Liu, B. (2017). Effects of inclusive leadership on employee voice behavior and team performance: The mediating role of caring ethical climate. *Frontiers in Communication*, *2*. https://doi.org/10.3389/FCOMM.2017.00008

Rashid, N. K. A., Lani, M. N., Ariffin, E. H., Mohamad, Z., & Ismail, I. R. (2023). Community engagement and social innovation through knowledge transfer: Micro evidence from Setiu Fishermen in Terengganu, Malaysia. *Journal of the Knowledge Economy*. https://doi.org/10.1007/S13132-023-01102-5

Reay, T., Jaskiewicz, P., & Hinings, C. R. (Bob). (2015). How family, business, and community logics shape family firm behavior and "rules of the game" in an organizational field. Http://Dx.Doi.Org/10.1177/0894486515577513, *28*(4), 292–311. https://doi.org/10.1177/0894486515577513

Roitman, J. (2022). The ends of perpetual crisis. *Global Discourse*, *12*(3–4), 692–696. https://doi.org/10.1332/204378921X16376650676641

Rowley, S., Pineault, L., & Dickson, M. (2021). Crisis demands leadership, so does our research. *Industrial and Organizational Psychology*, *14*(1–2), 112–116. https://doi.org/10.1017/IOP.2021.18

Schau, H. J., Muñiz, A. M., & Arnould, E. J. (2009). How brand community practices create value. *Journal of Marketing*, *73*(5), 30–51. https://doi.org/10.1509/JMKG.73.5.30

Schein, E. (2010). *Organizational Culture and Leadership*. Jossey-Bass. https://books.google.no/books?id=Mnres2PlFLMC&printsec=frontcover&source=gbs_ge_summary_r&cad=0%23v=onepage&q&f=false#v=onepage&q&f=false

Sen, S., & Bhattacharya, C. B. (2001). Does doing good always lead to doing better? Consumer reactions to corporate social responsibility. Https://Doi.Org/10.1509/Jmkr.38.2.225.18838, *38*(2), 225–243. https://doi.org/10.1509/JMKR.38.2.225.18838

Simola, S. (2003). Ethics of justice and care in corporate crisis management. *Journal of Business Ethics*, *46*(4), 351–361. https://doi.org/10.1023/A:1025607928196

Sparrowe, R. T. (2005). Authentic leadership and the narrative self. *Leadership Quarterly, 16*(3), 419–439. https://doi.org/10.1016/J.LEAQUA.2005.03.004

Standiford, T. C., Davuluri, K., Trupiano, N., et al. (2021). Physician leadership during the COVID-19 pandemic: An emphasis on the team, well-being and leadership reasoning. *BMJ Leader, 5*(1), 20–25. https://doi.org/10.1136/LEADER-2020-000344

Steenkamp, H., & Rensburg, R. (2019). CSR on display: Using spectacles and storytelling as stakeholder engagement mechanisms. *Communitas, 24*, 1–19. https://doi.org/10.18820/24150525/COMM.V24.2

Svedin, L. (2011). *Ethics and Crisis Management.* https://books.google.com/books?hl=en&lr=&id=4QAoDwAAQBAJ&oi=fnd&pg=PP1&dq=Svedin+2011+leadership&ots=PQdk7bCNLc&sig=FnzJmRcdLujZF5cqBaEd5kuUAi4

Swilling, M. (2013). Economic crisis, long waves and the sustainability transition: An African perspective. *Environmental Innovation and Social Transition.* www.sciencedirect.com/science/article/pii/S22104224120 0055X?casa_token=PdT_TYcIl1MAAAAA:BatjfVzv4J8A0JikliXgrQ8z C04Kr4v90V950Hid3b9MjMravEu-e1huDI0cFN8MzfHWWtDKvA

Swilling, M. (2019). Growth, sustainability and dematerialisation: Resource use options for South Africa 2019. In *sustainabilityinstitute.net.* www.sustainabil ityinstitute.net/wp-content/uploads/2020/01/submission-to-the-scenarios-2019-projectupdatednov07.pdf

Thoms, J. C. (2008). Ethical integrity in leadership and organizational moral culture. Leadership, 4(4), 419–442. https://doi.org/10.1177/17427150 08095189

Treviño, L. K., Brown, M., & Hartman, L. P. (2003). A qualitative investigation of perceived executive ethical leadership: Perceptions from inside and out- side the executive suite. *Human Relations, 56*(1), 5–37. https://doi.org/10.1177/0018726703056001448

Tucker, A. L., & Singer, S. J. (2015). The effectiveness of management-by-walking-around: A randomized field study. *Production and Operations Management, 24*(2), 253–271. https://doi.org/10.1111/POMS.12226

van Vugt, M., & Ronay, R. (2013). The evolutionary psychology of leadership. Http://Dx.Doi.Org/10.1177/2041386613493635, 4(1), 74–95. https://doi.org/10.1177/2041386613493635

Williams, T., Gruber, D., … K. S.-A. of, & 2017, undefined. (2017). Organizational response to adversity: Fusing crisis management and resili- ence research streams. *Journals.Aom.Org, 11*(2), 733–769. https://doi.org/10.5465/annals.2015.0134

Acknowledgments

Writing this work has been a decade-long journey. Our first foray into connecting our empirical pieces into meaningful narrative began with a Big Idea piece in *Harvard Business Review* in 2021. We're indebted to Laura Amico, our editor at *HBR* who saw the idea's potential and showed us how to execute it. Ronald Riggio's vision drew us to Cambridge University Press. We deeply thank him and the Elements *Leadership* editorial board for their enthusiastic support.

We owe our deepest gratitude to those we interviewed – those living through the crises that we study, at times to great personal, professional, and community risk. For example, Merrill Fernando, who passed away before this work was published, gave hours of his time on his 90th birthday as he was receiving the Business for Peace Award to tell stories well beyond what our research needed. The world is a dimmer place without Merrill, and we hope his stories of leadership help his memory be more widely known. The Oslo Business and Peace Foundation and its founder Per Saxegaard were instrumental in setting interviews with Fernando, Zaki Khouri, Paul Polman, and others highlighted in our research.

We also have a large network of co-authors who have gathered and analyzed empirical research by our sides over the last fifteen years. These include Kristian Hoeschler, Tim Fort, Brian Ganson, John Forrer, Angelika Rettberg, Ben Miller, Rina Alluri, Peer Schouten, Jennifer Oetzel, Jay Joseph, Sarah Cechvala, Cindy Horst, Øystein Rolandsen, Yass Alkafaji, Juan Pablo Medina Bickel, Benedicte Bull, Drew Marcantonio, Tor Brodtkorb, and Jamal Maalouf. Aida El Khatib and Abegail Morata at American University of Sharjah graciously provided time to do this research. We wrote much of the Element in Shelter Island, NY and thank residents for their support, particularly Trish Anzalone, who always had words of encouragement. We also deeply thank an anonymous reviewer, Lisa DiMona, Brad Wetzler, Scott Carney, Ryan Highland, and Joanne Murphy for feedback on early drafts.

Cambridge Elements

Leadership

Ronald E. Riggio
Claremont Mckenna College

Ronald E. Riggio, Ph.D., is the Henry R. Kravis Professor of Leadership and Organisational Psychology and former Director of the Kravis Leadership Institute at Claremont Mckenna College. Dr. Riggio is a psychologist and leadership scholar with over a dozen authored or edited books and more than 150 articles/book chapters. He has worked as a consultant and serves on multiple editorial boards.

Susan E. Murphy
University of Edinburgh

Susan E. Murphy is Chair in Leadership Development at the University of Edinburgh Business School. She has published numerous articles and book chapters on leadership, leadership development, and mentoring. Susan was formerly Director of the School of Strategic Leadership Studies at James Madison University and Professor of Leadership Studies. Prior to that, she served as faculty and associate director of the Henry R. Kravis Leadership Institute at Claremont Mckenna College. She also serves on the editorial board of The Leadership Quarterly.

Georgia Sorenson
University of Cambridge

The late Georgia Sorenson, Ph.D., was the James MacGregor Burns Leadership Scholar at the Moller Institute and Moller By-Fellow of Churchill College at Cambridge University. Before coming to Cambridge, she founded the James MacGregor Burns Academy of Leadership at the University of Maryland, where she was Distinguished Research Professor. An architect of the leadership studies field, Dr. Sorenson has authored numerous books and refereed journal articles.

Advisory Board

Micha Popper, *University of Haifa*
Terry Price, *University of Richmond*
Krish Raval, *University of Oxford*
Roni Reiter-Palmon, *University of Nebraska*
Birgit Schyns, *Durham University*
Gillian Secrett, *University of Cambridge*
Nicholas Warner, *Claremont McKenna College*

About the Series

Cambridge Elements in Leadership is multi- and inter-disciplinary and will have broad appeal for leadership courses in Schools of Business, Education, Engineering, Public Policy, and in the Social Sciences and Humanities.

Cambridge Elements ≡

Leadership

Elements in the series

Leadership Studies and the Desire for Shared Agreement: A Narrative Inquiry
Stan Amaladas

Leading the Future of Technology: The Vital Role of Accessible Technologies
Rebecca LaForgia

Cultural Dynamics and Leadership: An Interpretive Approach
Nathan W. Harter

There Is More Than One Way To Lead: The Charismatic, Ideological, And Pragmatic (CIP) Theory Of Leadership
Samuel T. Hunter and Jeffrey B. Lovelace

Leading for Innovation: Leadership Actions to Enhance Follower Creativity
Michael D. Mumford, Tanner R. Newbold, Mark Fichtel, and Samantha England

The Hazards of Great Leadership: Detrimental Consequences of Leader Exceptionalism
James K. Beggan, Scott T. Allison, and George R. Goethals

The Gift of Transformative Leaders
Nathan O. Hatch

Questioning Leadership
Michael Harvey

Ethical Leadership in Conflict and Crisis: Evidence from Leaders on How to Make More Peaceful, Sustainable, and Profitable Communities
Jason Miklian and John E. Katsos

A full series listing is available at: www.cambridge.org/CELE

Printed in the United States
by Baker & Taylor Publisher Services